JACK RUSSELL
Terrier

AN OWNER'S GUIDE

Dedication

This book is dedicated to my friend Clive Hoyle, a master breeder of Welsh cobs and working Jack Russell Terriers under his prefix 'Llangybi'. I thank him for showing me the way with Llangybi Mister Chips, the most maddening but loveable Terrier I've ever had, and I've had a few!

Robert Killick

Robert is a country man who, as a boy, lived in Surrey and Somerset, surrounded by dogs of many breeds, especially Terriers, Gundogs and Hounds. After a career in the theatre he moved to a secluded farm in wild west Wales 35 years ago to breed sheep, Welsh Terriers and Wire Haired Fox Terriers. For many years, he exhibited dogs with a degree of success and also has a Judge's Diploma (Credit). Robert has worked as a journalist and columnist for *Our Dogs* and has written features and short stories for *Dogs Today*. He has also contributed columns in American, Swedish and Australian publications. He is also the author of several books for HarperCollins, including volumes on dog showing and dog breeds. He lives with his calm wife Jo (She who Pulls the Strings), a lazy, unmoving Mini Wire haired Dachshund, Herr Egon von Klick and the exuberant Hunt Jack Russell Mister Chips.

David Taylor B.V.M.S., F.R.C.V.S., F.Z.S.

David Taylor is a veterinary surgeon and author who has worked with a wide spectrum of animal species for many years. Founder of the International Zoo Veterinary Group, he has had patients ranging from the King of Spain's Giant Pandas to gorillas in West Africa and killer whales with frostbite in Iceland. He has written over 100 books on animal matters including many best-selling dog books and seven volumes of autobiography. The latter formed the basis for three series of the BBC television drama *One by One*. He lives in Hertfordshire, England.

JACK RUSSELL
Terrier

AN OWNER'S GUIDE

Robert Killick

**Healthcare by
David Taylor**

First published in 2009 by
Collins, an imprint of
HarperCollins Publishers
77–85 Fulham Palace Road
Hammersmith, London W6 8JB

The Collins website address is:
www.collins.co.uk

11 10
6 5 4 3 2

A catalogue record for this book is available from the British Library.

Created by: SP Creative Design
Editor: Heather Thomas
Designer: Rolando Ugolini
Photography: All photographs by Rolando Ugolini with the exception of the following: pages 17, 21,49 and 94 (Alan Seymour) and pages 29, 87, 89 and 91 (Alan Walker)

ISBN: 978-0-00-727430-7

Printed and bound by Printing Express Ltd., Hong Kong

Acknowledgements
The Breed Standard on pages 22–23 is reproduced by kind permission of the Kennel Club. The Breed Standard on pages 20–21 is reproduced by kind permission of the Jack Russell Terrier Club of Great Britain. The publishers would also like to thank the following individuals for their help in producing the photography in this book: Barbara Hall, Alex Browne (Afinley) and their dogs and Jack and Chloe Smith and their dogs. The author would like to thank the following: James Crowley, AKC, Caroline Kisko and her PA James Skinner of The Kennel Club, Kevin Horkin of the Pet Role Trust, Adrian Guthrie of the Jack Russell Terrier Club of Great Britain and Bill Roache, owned by four Jacks. Also Jack Russells Online for their description of the breed.

Note: The section on docking is only a summary of the regulations and, as such, neither the author nor the publishers can take responsibility for its accuracy. Contact DEFRA for further details. We are grateful to the Council for Docked Breeds for their help in compiling the new docking regulations.

Note: Dogs are referred to as 'he' throughout to avoid 'he'/'she' each time or the rather impersonal 'it'. This reflects no bias towards males, and both sexes are equally valuable and easy to train.

Contents

Foreword

I feel well placed to write this foreword and was delighted to have been asked. The first thing that makes me suitable is my Jack Russell experience. Everyone knows how demanding they are and to have one is a challenge – well, I have four! Each one is totally different, in your face, bright as a button, ahead of the game and completely beguiling. I would not be without them. Secondly, I am suitable through knowing the author, Robert Killick. For some years we have worked together on dog charity projects at Crufts and it is not only his love of dogs but also his encyclopedic knowledge of them that has enabled him to write seven books. He is the right man to write this book and I commend it to anyone who wants to know the real Jack Russell.

Bill Roache MBE

Introduction

The Jack Russell Terrier is one of the most important Terrier breeds because it has scarcely changed since its beginnings 150 years ago. Early photos and paintings show this to be true; indeed a photo of my dishevelled Jack Russell could be the litter brother to Trinity Jim, a famous Jack of around 1901. In this book we will present the quintessential modern Jack Russell from puppyhood through to adulthood.

I will be using the words 'Jack Russell' because the average member of the public does not know or, I suspect, care about the split in the breed. Whether he is called a Parson Russell Terrier or a Jack Russell, the names are synonymous with a happy, small, vibrant dog whose fame has spread through Europe, Australia and America as a worker and showdog.

Arguments rage about this Terrier, particularly his size, but a real Jack Russell is a running machine, slim, muscular with legs in proportion to his body – the short-legged round Terrier is not a proper Jack Russell.

Of all the many Terriers I have owned and bred in 35 years, my Jack Russell is the most intelligent and affectionate dog I've ever had – his zest for life is remarkable. He is not noisy or quarrelsome but he is self-willed and not easy to train. However, success will reward your patience and kindness. In the home he is good with children, playful and amusing, and, as a bonus, he is a great guard dog – no sound escapes him. As a country dog, he will walk you until you fall over and then want more. As a working Terrier he has no equal, being feisty, courageous and persistent, and yet he is flexible and will be at home in the town or city with sufficient exercise and mental stimulation.

The breed's creator, Reverend John (Jack) Russell, was a legend in his lifetime, his Terriers were his legacy and they are a legend in our time.

Robert Killick

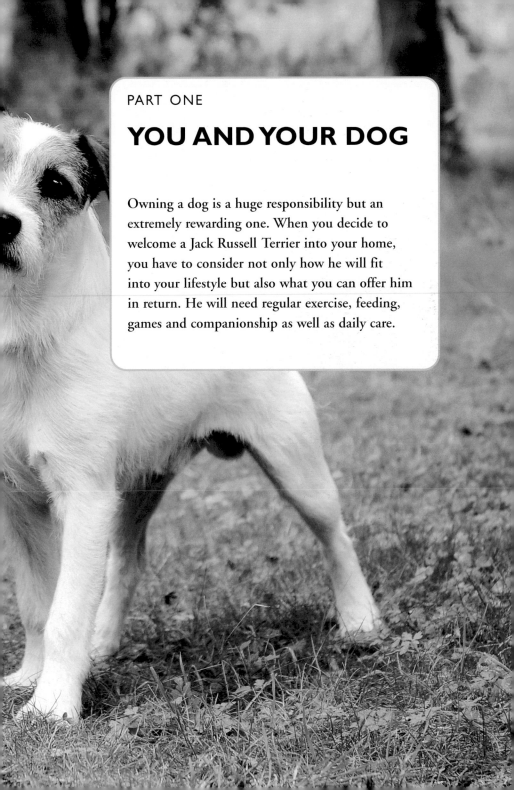

PART ONE

YOU AND YOUR DOG

Owning a dog is a huge responsibility but an extremely rewarding one. When you decide to welcome a Jack Russell Terrier into your home, you have to consider not only how he will fit into your lifestyle but also what you can offer him in return. He will need regular exercise, feeding, games and companionship as well as daily care.

Chapter 1

History of the breed

There are two strains of the same breed, which are prevalent in Great Britain. The Parson Russell Terrier, which is officially recognized by the UK Kennel Club, is, largely speaking, a show dog and pet, although many are working dogs. The other strain, which is more numerous, is simply the Jack Russell Terrier, a working Terrier and also a pet, as recognized and supported by the Jack Russell Terrier Club of Great Britain. Both have their roots in the same stock, that of the Reverend John (Jack) Russell (1795–1883), who, from 1815 until his death, developed his own strain of hunt Terriers which suited his style of hunting and the terrain over which he hunted.

Evolution of dogs

We will never know exactly how, why and when wolves morphed themselves into domestic dogs; it was part of the evolutionary process and could have been over a period of 500,000 years or more. Those of us blessed with a vivid imagination can picture in our minds a family of primitive men sitting round a fire eating the results of the day's hunt. The glittering eyes of wolves can be seen watching from the bushes, waiting for the bones that will be tossed into the undergrowth. Wolves, being intelligent, realized that primitive man was a source of food, and because they went hunting as a group, they would skulk along behind the humans in the hope that when they killed their prey there might be enough left over for them.

Early Man may have thought of wolves as a source of food – they were edible, especially when young. Primitive children may have liked the look of wolf puppies when they were brought back to the cave as living store food, and perhaps they found that the puppies kept them warm at night, so they kept them and became attached to them. Slowly, over many years, the two species came to trust each other. Primitive man realized that domesticated wolves could help him find his prey and then kill it. With their superior hearing, they also made good guard dogs, warning of the approach of other humans, animals or predators, and this type probably became sheep and

Opposite: Both the Parson Russell Terrier and the Jack Russell Terrier make excellent ratters, and they love to scent and hunt equally in city gardens or in the countryside.

cattle dogs as men became agronomists. The early association between primitive man and wolves has been proved by the discovery of wolf bones, which were found buried with human ones, dating back 500,000 years.

Selective breeding

We know that breeds of dog were bred for specific purposes even in ancient times and were respected in many early civilizations in the Middle East, ancient Egypt and China. An enormous number of ancient artefacts depicting dogs have been found in what are now Iraq and Iran as well as the Egyptian pyramids. It is not easy to recognize which breeds are portrayed in these ancient sites, mainly because they were not as sharply defined as they are today. Canophilists can find aspects in early statues and frescos of heavy war dogs, slim hunting dogs and small companion animals, but they seldom identify Terriers because they probably did not exist in any way as we know them nowadays.

The spread of dogs

There is no mystery as to how breeds of dogs were distributed around Europe. Armies, moving on foot for thousands of miles, were usually accompanied by their own dogs and captured indigenous dogs as they travelled. They needed war dogs, watch dogs and herding dogs to control the herds of animals they took with them. During campaigns, invasions and occupations, they left behind and sold some of these dogs. Another mode of distribution was by coastal sea traders,

notably the Phoenicians who sailed the Mediterranean and reached the coast of the British Isles. Dogs were probably sold and may have survived shipwrecks, later mixing and breeding with the local canine population. Sheep traders from Europe also brought dogs to Britain, which they would have left behind or perhaps traded with the locals.

Advent of the Terrier

The Terrier was most likely a late addition to the British Isles. Early man saw rats as a food source but later, when he had discovered how to keep the crops he had grown, they became a nuisance and he needed smaller wolf-like dogs to catch and kill them. For reasons not fully understood, every breed of Terrier

History of Terriers

Very little was written on Terriers in ancient times, although Oppian wrote in the third century of small dogs used by the rough natives of Britain to scent and hunt game. Later, in 1486, Dame Juliana Berners mentioned 'terours' among other breeds of 'dogges' in her *Boke of St Albans*. Dr Johannes Caius presented terriers as we would recognize them today in his book on dogs, *De Canibus Britannicis* (1570). In 1686, Richard Blome described the working Terrier, which was indicative of a change in the attitude of huntsmen and the development of Terriers.

emanates from the British Isles, and even though a few new breeds have been developed, they came from British breeds originally. The German Hunt Terrier (Jagdterrier) and the Czech Cesky Terrier are two examples. For millennia, small, feisty dogs of no particular type were kept around British homesteads to control rats and other small mammals considered vermin. These dogs doubled as farm guards. We can only assume that it was from an amalgam of many breeds that the first Terrier types evolved.

It is a Jack Russell's instinct to hunt and to dig. Like most other Terrier breeds, these dogs were developed to keep down vermin.

In pre-medieval and medieval times, the aristocracy hunted deer for pleasure and the larder, so the development of hounds was their priority. Terriers were for the peasantry and interested the nobility only when they were engaged in dog fights, bull baiting and badger hunting. Medieval laws even forbade peasants from owning hunting dogs and disabled any suspect dogs to prevent them being used for deer hunting. Gundogs became a necessity when guns were introduced – Setters were used to indicate where the birds were, and Retrievers to bring back the dead.

Fox hunting

This sport started to be popular during the fifteenth century when hunters discovered the pleasure of a long run on horseback in pursuit of the fox. They divided their time between stag hunting for food and fox hunting for pleasure and used the same staghounds for both. They soon realized, however, that the staghounds were too heavy and slow for hunting the fox and replaced them with lighter, faster animals.

Because foxes were adept at hiding, the lowly Terrier came into his own. Hitherto the peasant's yard dog, he was now valued by the aristocracy. He was small with a wonderful sense of smell, feisty and courageous enough to go to earth and either mark where the fox was lying by barking or force him to leave the safety of his lair. If the former was the case and the Terrier was marking the fox, he was expected to keep barking, so that the huntsmen could dig out the fox, release it, give it a head start and then pursue it again.

Parson Jack Russell did not want his Terriers to kill foxes, although most were quite capable of doing so; they needed to defend themselves against a fox that was desperately trying to escape. Therefore a Terrier had to be brave and sufficiently skilled to take on a fox fighting for its life in darkness in an unfamiliar, small underground chamber.

Many huntsmen began to develop their own strain of Terriers. In the early days, they favoured the ubiquitous Black and Tan Terrier, which although now extinct is still present genetically in many familiar breeds. The colour white was introduced, because in bad light and heavy undergrowth the hounds could easily mistake a dark-coloured dog for the fox, and many a fine Terrier was killed in that way.

John Russell

Only with knowledge of the Reverend John (Jack) Russell, his life and times can we have a better understanding of the breed that carries his name and has done so for more than 150 years. The rural society in which he was born and lived was one of poverty, with many livelihoods dependent on the whims of land owners. Work was long and arduous and there was little to do in the way of entertainment. Hunting was a way of life, and the very existence of a hunt could sustain whole communities.

Early life

John Russell was born in 1795 in Devonshire, and from boyhood showed an exceptional interest in the countryside and animals. His father, a well-known hunting parson, who, at one time, kept a pack of hounds, encouraged his son to follow in his footsteps. At that time it was not unusual for men of the cloth to be keen on hunting. Indeed, many had their own packs, and they were

often admired by their parishioners and overlooked by the church hierarchy.

Young John Russell was a tough, strong country lad, who was not easily put down and was always ready to fight his corner, which was just as well for his second school, Blundell's, a public school in Tiverton, Devon, had a harsh regime, and bullying was rife. He kept ferrets and in his spare time would go ratting for local farmers, who were amused by the boy's keenness and agreed to keep four-and-a-half couple of hounds (nine hounds) on his behalf.

Today's Jack Russells are all descended from the original Terriers owned by the Reverend John Russell in the nineteenth century. Feisty and fun-loving, these dogs make great family pets as well as being superb workers.

At Oxford University, Russell was not interested in cock fighting and heavy drinking like the other young gentlemen undergraduates. Instead, he used every opportunity to hunt with the best packs. Foxhunting became the story of his life, and he was obsessed with hunting until his eighties, riding phenomenal distances to join a famous hunt.

The Jack Russell Terrier

The tale of how Russell found his first Terrier is well known, but it will lose nothing in re-telling. He was taking an early morning walk in Oxford when he saw the local milkman delivering milk with a white Terrier at his heel. Russell fell for the dog and could not rest until he had bought her. Her name was Trump and she became the foundation bitch of his kennel.

A famous Terrier man

In 1873, Russell became one of the founder members of the Kennel Club, but although he showed dogs for a short period he believed that dogs bred for the show ring would lose their working characteristics and he was only interested in function. Writing about him in 1904, H. Compton stated, 'For where shall you find any Terrier strain, or for that matter any strain of dogs, as honoured and renowned as that of the Devonshire Parson whose distaste for show dogs was almost as profound as his admiration for working ones'.

Although he was said to be 'the father of Fox Terriers', which he kept within his own stud, some people claimed he would buy any likely looking Terrier and breed from it. Unfortunately, we'll never know the truth because few of his records have survived, but, to use a stockman's expression, 'he had an eye for a dog' and by a process of selective breeding became the most famous Terrier man in Britain. His fame extended far and wide, not only for his hunting prowess but also for his knowledge of country matters.

The Reverend John (Jack) Russell died on 28th April 1883, and, to illustrate how greatly he was esteemed and loved, over 1,000 people attended his funeral, including 24 clergymen, the mayor of Barnstaple and many hunting celebrities. Even the Prince of Wales sent a wreath of wild flowers celebrating Parson Jack's love of the countryside.

Supporters of the breed

Two other men who should be named because of their support of Parson Jack and his strain of Terriers are Arthur Heinemann and Squire Nicholas Snow of Oare. Heinemann acquired his original stock of Jack Russell Terriers from the squire, and his kennel woman, Annie Rawle, was the granddaughter of the Parson's kennel manager, Will Rawle. It was Annie who managed Heinemann's kennels when the master was serving in World War I. Heinemann was also an obsessive huntsman and a student of Parson Jack's breeding methods. He wrote the original Standard for the breed, which has been preserved virtually intact to modern times. He also built up a strong kennel of Terriers, and on his death in 1930 his stock passed to Annie Rawle, thereby ensuring the continuation of the type.

Using the Parson's dogs as patterns, the early show enthusiasts began to 'improve' on the originals. They developed their dogs to win in the show ring, but, in the view of many hunting people, they changed the priorities, making perceived beauty the most important criteria instead of function.

They thought that the show Terrier would never be called upon to prove his metal in the field and therefore was not worthy of consideration.

Today's working Jack Russell Terrier is a game little dog with all the instincts of his ancestors. He loves to dig and hunt.

Fox Terrier Club

At the time the generic name for Terriers bred to run with Fox Hounds was 'Fox Terrier', and even the Parson's dogs were alluded to as Fox Terriers. Indeed, to some he was the father of the breed. However, other gentlemen, wishing to stabilize the breed, created the Fox Terrier Club and sought recognition from the Kennel Club, which they achieved in 1872. Parson Jack Russell would have none of it and would not register his strain of Terriers with the Kennel Club, believing that it would dilute their hunting qualities. Many enthusiasts followed him, continuing to breed their working terriers in the time-honoured way – only from dogs that showed prowess in the hunting field – and called them Jack Russell Terriers.

However, in 1894, Heinemann formed the Devon & Somerset Badger Club, which later changed its name to the Parson Jack Russell Club and became one of the 28 clubs affiliated to the Fox Terrier Club in the 1930s. Sadly, they folded just before World War II.

By the turn of the century, dog shows were becoming very popular, and at the same time the Kennel Club's registered Smooth Fox Terriers became the most popular Terrier exhibits. However, in some litters of Smooths, Wire-haired puppies appeared, which, although they were not favoured at the time, overtook the Smooths in popularity several years later. From photographs of the time it is easy to see that the Fox Terriers were not so very different to those of today.

Popularity of the breed

The one major problem that has haunted the breed, since its superb working qualities were recognized, is the spread of what can only be described as 'counterfeit' Jack Russells, because few people adhered to a Standard. During World War II, food was scarce and it was difficult to feed kennels of dogs, so many were forced to close down and numerous dogs did not survive.

After the war, when the servicemen started returning home, there was a renewed demand for puppies, and many dog breeders, who were quick to seize the opportunity, began their operations again, producing so-called Jack Russell Terriers, which were actually a mish-mash of types.

Puppy farmers and backyard breeders, seeking only to make money, would mate any Terriers together and call the resultant progeny Jack Russells. Farmers bred Terriers with small sheepdogs and described the puppies as Jack Russells. Although some of these dogs could work foxes or rats with varying degrees of efficacy, in reality they bore little or no resemblance to the real thing, and their puppies would not reproduce the Jack Russell Terrier's characteristic type. Anyone with a scant knowledge of the breed could recognize major type faults, such as heads that were too wide, weak jaws, dogs that were too big around the chest, long coupled, short front legs (Queen Ann legs) with turned out stifles, together with a lack of balance and symmetry. Other faults occurring in some dogs might include protuberant eyes, incorrect coat texture and colour, big pricked ears and roached backs.

Jack Russell Terrier Club

In 1974 a group of Terrier enthusiasts gathered together to form the Jack Russell Terrier Club of Great Britain (JRTC of GB) and to write a Standard in an attempt to stabilize the breed. A constitution was drawn up, with rule No. 1 being 'To promote and preserve the working Terrier known as the Jack Russell'. To maintain the perceived difference between the working dog and the Kennel Club registered dog, Rule 2f of their constitution reads: 'History has shown that Kennel Club recognition to be detrimental to the physical structure and working capabilities of a variety of working breeds, therefore this club is opposed to the Kennel Club recognition of the Jack Russell Terrier'.

Parson Russell Club

Other enthusiasts, who wanted to show their dogs, followed a different path to their eventual recognition by the Kennel Club. In 1894, Heinemann formed the Devon & Somerset Badger Club, which later changed its name to the Parson Jack Russell Club and became one of the 28 clubs affiliated to the Fox Terrier Club in the 1930s. Sadly, they folded just before World War II but some breeders still clung to the old ideals of a terrier whose legs were long enough to allow him to run with the hounds, whose chest could be spanned and who was courageous and strong enough to face an angry fox in his lair. They thought, rightly or wrongly, that the only way to preserve the real

Jack Russell was to gain recognition from the Kennel Club and to have an official Standard for the breed.

Late in 1983 there was a rumour that supporters of a short-legged variety were to apply for recognition to the Kennel Club, so the enthusiasts for the show dogs, who believed their version was closer to the original, hurriedly formed the Parson Jack Russell Club and applied for recognition, which was refused. In 1990, after much controversy and several attempts, the new club received Kennel Club recognition and its eventual name was The Parson Russell Club.

The sizes of both strains of this intelligent Terrier are commensurate with running with hounds, going to earth and ratting.

The Breed Standards

These are detailed descriptions of ideal dogs within the breed. A Standard is not a blueprint because, as a living creature, no dog can replicate another. Instead, it is a guide to perfection. The perfect dog does not exist, which is why we strive to breed better dogs that are as close to the Standard as possible.

If you want a puppy for showing or breeding, you should immerse yourself in the breed and make a study of the Standard to familiarize yourself with its every nuance. A real insight into a breed is not gained overnight, nor does it matter how much theoretical knowledge you have – instead, it demands 'hands on' experience.

Note that the word 'type', as applied to dogs, can be confusing. If a dog is said to lack type it means that he lacks some of the characteristics that typify the breed. The precise meaning of the word is 'the hundreds of points which when put together makes one breed distinguishable from all others'. Type is contained within the Standard.

The Jack Russell Terrier (The Jack Russell Terrier Club of Great Britain Standard)

Characteristics The Terrier must present a lively, active and alert appearance with its fearless and happy disposition. It should be remembered that the Jack Russell is a working Terrier, and should retain these instincts. Nervousness, cowardice and over-aggression should be discouraged, and the dog should always appear confident.

General appearance A sturdy, tough Terrier, very much on its toes all the time. Measuring between 25cm (10in) and 37cm (15in) at the withers. The body length must be in proportion to the height, and it should present a compact, balanced image, always being in solid, hard condition.

Head Should be well balanced and in proportion to the body. The skull should be flat, of moderate width at the ears, narrowing to the eyes, There should be a defined stop, but not over-pronounced, The length of the muzzle from the nose to the stop should be slightly shorter than the distance from the stop to the occiput. The nose should be black. The jaw should be powerful and well boned with strongly muscled cheeks.

Eyes Should be almond-shaped, dark in colour and full of life and intelligence.

Ears Small V-shaped, drop ears carried forward close to the head and of moderate thickness.

Mouth Strong teeth with the upper set slightly overlapping the lower.

Neck Clean and muscular, of good length, gradually widening at the shoulder.

Forequarters The shoulders should be

sloping and well laid back, fine at points and clearly cut at the withers, Forelegs should be strong and straight boned with joints in correct alignment. Elbows hanging perpendicular to the body and working free of the sides.

Body The chest should be shallow, narrow and the front legs set not too widely apart giving an athletic rather than a heavy chested appearance. As a guide only, the chest should be small enough to be easily spanned behind the shoulders by average hands when the Terrier is in a fit, working condition. The back should be strong, straight and in comparison to the height of the Terrier, give a balanced image. The loin should be slightly arched.

Hindquarters Should be strong and muscular, well put together with good angulation and hand of stifle, giving plenty of drive and propulsion. Looking from behind the hocks must be straight.

Feet Round, hard padded of cat-like appearance, neither turning in nor out.

Tail Should be set rather high, carried gaily and in proportion to the body length, usually about 10cm (4in) long, providing a good handhold.

Coat Smooth, without being so sparse as not to provide a certain amount of protection from the elements and undergrowth. Rough or broken-coated without being woolly.

Colour White should predominate with tan, black or brown Markings. Brindle markings are unacceptable.

Gait Movement should be free, lively and well co-ordinated with straight action in front and behind.

The Parson Russell Terrier (The Kennel Club Standard)

General appearance Workmanlike, active and agile, built for speed and endurance. Overall picture of balance and flexibility. Honourable scars permissible.

Characteristics Essentially a working terrier with ability and conformation to go to ground and run with hounds.

Temperament Bold and friendly.

Head and skull Flat, moderately broad, gradually narrowing to the eyes. Shallow stop. Length of nose to stop slightly shorter than from stop to occiput. Nose black.

Eyes Almond shaped, fairly deep set, dark, keen expression.

Ears Small, V-shaped, dropping forward, carried close to head, tip of ear to reach corner of the eye, fold not to appear above top of skull. Leather of moderate thickness.

Mouth Jaws strong, muscular. Teeth with a perfect, regular and complete scissor bite, i.e. upper teeth closely overlapping lower teeth and set square to the jaws.

Neck Clean, muscular, of good length gradually widening to shoulders.

Forequarters Shoulders long and sloping, well laid back. Cleanly cut at withers. Legs strong, must be straight with joints turning neither in nor out. Elbows close to body, working free of the sides.

Body Ribs not over-sprung. Chest of moderate depth, capable of being spanned behind the shoulders by average hands. Back strong and straight. Loin slightly arched. Well balanced. Overall length slightly longer than height from withers to ground.

Hindquarters Strong, muscular with good angulation and bend of stifle. Hocks set low and rear pasterns parallel giving plenty of drive.

Feet Compact with firm pads, turning neither in nor out.

Tail (Before change in law 2007) Customarily docked with length complimenting the body while providing a good handhold. Strong, straight, moderately high set carried well up on the move. Undocked: Of moderate length and as straight as possible, giving a general balance to the dog, thick at the root and tapering towards the end. Moderately high set carried well up on the move.

Gait/movement Free striding, well co-ordinated, straight action front and behind.

Coat Naturally harsh, close and dense, whether rough or smooth. Belly and undersides coated. Skin must be thick and loose.

Colour Entirely white, or predominantly white with tan, lemon or black markings,

or any combination of these colours, preferably confined to the head and/or root of tail.

Size Ideal height at withers: dogs 35cm (14in): bitches 33cm (13in). 2.5cm (1in) above or below is acceptable.

Faults Any departure from the foregoing points should be considered a fault and the seriousness with which the fault should be regarded should be in exact proportion to its degree.

Note: Male animals should have two apparently normal testicles fully descended into the scrotum.

© The Kennel Club

Docking and the law

A ban on tail docking came into effect in the UK early in the spring of 2007. No dogs can be docked in Scotland, but there are exceptions for certain breeds in England and Wales. Dogs may only be docked by a qualified veterinary surgeon if they are convinced that the dog will be used for work, and even then they have the right to refuse. The puppy should be presented before it is five days old, the vet must have view of the puppies' dam and the sight of a document signed by the applicant claiming the puppy will be used for pest control. Further proof will be required by the vet in the shape of a shotgun licence issued to the owner of the dog or a letter from a gamekeeper or land owner with shooting rights, a person representing the National Working Terrier Federation (and other responsible persons connected with vermin control) who will state they know the person whose puppy is to be docked and they have been used on property owned or managed by them.

In England, Terriers of any type or combination of types can be shown.

In Wales, the law regarding docked Terriers is different and is applicable only to the following: Jack Russell Terriers, Cairn Terriers, Lakeland Terriers and Norfolk Terriers but not combinations of breeds.

A dog docked before 28th March 2007 in Wales and 6th April in England may continue to be shown in the UK throughout its natural life.

A dog docked on or after the above dates, no matter where it was docked, may not be shown in England and Wales where the public is charged for admission.

However, dogs legally docked in England and Wales can be shown where the public is charged for entry, so long as it is to be shown in a way to demonstrate its working ability and not for conformity to a Standard. A dog legally docked in England, Wales, Northern Ireland or overseas may be shown in Scotland.

Warning: If a person is found guilty of an offence under the Animal Welfare Act 2006 (England) the penalty can be a fine of £20,000 or imprisonment of 51 weeks or both.

The Parson Russell Terrier

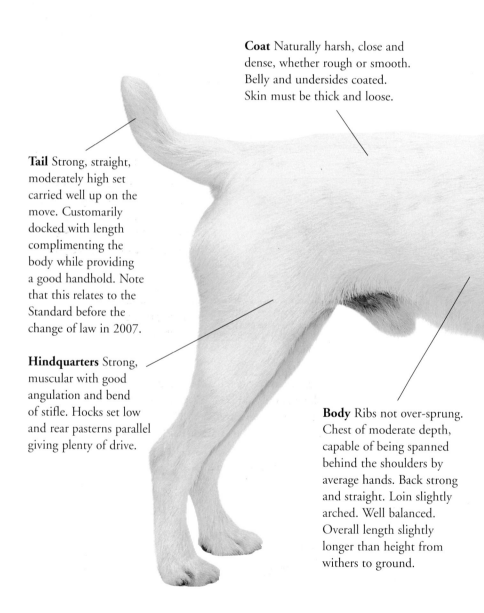

Coat Naturally harsh, close and dense, whether rough or smooth. Belly and undersides coated. Skin must be thick and loose.

Tail Strong, straight, moderately high set carried well up on the move. Customarily docked with length complimenting the body while providing a good handhold. Note that this relates to the Standard before the change of law in 2007.

Hindquarters Strong, muscular with good angulation and bend of stifle. Hocks set low and rear pasterns parallel giving plenty of drive.

Body Ribs not over-sprung. Chest of moderate depth, capable of being spanned behind the shoulders by average hands. Back strong and straight. Loin slightly arched. Well balanced. Overall length slightly longer than height from withers to ground.

Ears Small, V-shaped, dropping forward, carried close to head, tip of ear to reach corner of the eye, fold not to appear above top of skull. Leather of moderate thickness.

Eyes Almond shaped, fairly deep set, dark, keen expression.

Mouth Jaws strong, muscular. Teeth with a perfect, regular and complete scissor bite, i.e. upper teeth closely overlapping lower teeth and set square to the jaws.

Neck Clean, muscular, of good length gradually widening to shoulders.

Forequarters Shoulders long and sloping, well laid back. Cleanly cut at withers. Legs strong, must be straight with joints turning neither in nor out. Elbows close to body, working free of the sides.

Feet Compact with firm pads, turning neither in nor out.

Chapter 2

Acquiring a puppy

The best time to collect your puppy is when he is about eight or nine weeks old. At this stage, he should be mature enough to settle into his new home with minimal stress and upheaval for both of you. Start socializing him immediately – learning about the world will help make him more confident and less likely to experience behaviour problems later on.

Responsible dog ownership

Introducing a puppy into your home is a big step, particularly if it is the first time you have owned a dog. However, before rushing into buying a dog, it is of prime importance that you decide whether you can manage the newcomer. Do you have enough time to house train, socialize and exercise him? Have you considered the cost of feeding him and sudden expenses you may incur, such as vet's bills?

Remember that a dog is a sentient creature. He is also a pack animal and is happiest when he is surrounded by his family – human or dog. It is not fair on a young puppy, or an adult dog for that matter, to leave him alone whilst you and members of your family are out at work for many hours each day. It is not in their nature to be alone, and, almost

certainly, they will get into some sort of mischief from sheer boredom, such as chewing the furniture, their bedding or your cushions. So you should think extremely carefully before deciding to welcome a dog into your household, especially an active dog with a working temperament, such as a Jack Russell.

Which style is right for you?

Because there are two styles of the breed – the Parson Russell Terrier and the Jack Russell Terrier – you must consider which type you want. This will depend on what you expect to do with the adult dog.

Parson Russell type

If you want to show and breed from your dog eventually under the Kennel Club (KC) rules, you will need to buy a puppy from a breeder who breeds Parson Russell Terriers, registers them with the Kennel Club and who adheres as closely as possible to the written Standard (see page 22). Only dogs that are registered with the Kennel Club can be shown at

Opposite: This puppy looks adorable but before you acquire one, consider whether it is the right decision for you and your family.

their shows, and only puppies born of KC registered parents can be registered.

Jack Russell type

If you are not interested in exhibiting dogs in the formal atmosphere of Kennel Club (KC) shows, you prefer country pursuits and do not wish to register any puppies that you may breed, you can buy your puppy from a breeder who breeds under the Jack Russell Terrier Club of Great Britain's (JRTC of GB) rules and Breed Standard. Their dogs will be known as Working Jack Russells or Hunt Jack Russells. You will still be allowed to show your dog at KC Companion Shows as well as the Terrier shows staged by agriculture societies or the local hunt.

Differences between the types

After reading this, you would be forgiven for asking: 'So what is the difference between the two types?' In truth, not a lot, but there is a difference in height. The reason is that the working Terrier has to work the earths that are available: small Terriers fit small holes and big

Terriers do not. If you study both the Standards, you will see that:
- Both types should be capable of the work for which they were developed
- Their chests should be spannable by average-sized hands
- They should be able to run 20–30 miles a day or more with Foxhounds
- They should be brave enough to enter a fox's earth and face an angry fox.

I do not think that just because the Kennel Club has recognized the breed the hunting instinct has been diluted. It may happen in 100 years' time, but other Terrier breeds that have not been bred for work since World War I will still have a go if trained. It is doubtful if the genetic structure of instinct can be changed in just a few years.

The problem is that if a breeder has a really fine KC registered dog, which is winning a great deal at the championship shows, then it is unlikely that they will risk putting him to fox, so he will never have the opportunity to prove his metal in the field.

There is also a train of thought that a puppy from working stock will not be as good a pet as one from show stock. However, the Jack Russell or Parson Russell, whatever you call him, is one of the most adaptable Terriers. He is highly intelligent and will adapt to all the situations in which he finds himself.

Sourcing a puppy

Before we consider the best sources for Jack Russell puppies, here is a word of warning. Because of the bad mixed breeding and the over-production of

Activities

The Kennel Club allows non-registered dogs to participate in certain activities, such as Flyball, Obedience, Agility and Heelwork to Music. Because of their intelligence, energy and strength, Jack Russells are able to perform very well in all these disciplines.

'counterfeit' Jack Russells, the following sources should always be avoided:

- Buying from a man in the pub
- Buying from a puppy farmer
- Buying from a white van in a motorway car park
- Buying from a dog dealer
- Buying from a pet shop.

If something should go wrong after the sale – for instance, the puppy is ill or shows a genetic anomaly – you will have no redress and will probably never see the first, third and fourth people listed above ever again. The second and fifth sources will still be there, but they will not be of any help if you do experience some problems.

Puppies love to play together, and by going to a breeder's home you can observe them interacting with each other and their mother and get an idea of their character.

If you see puppies advertised in local or free newspapers, you should be wary if several breeds are listed within the same advertisement. These small ads are usually placed by puppy farmers and/or dog dealers. The same advice applies to puppies that are advertised on the Internet. If you see an advertisement exclusively for Jack Russell puppies and, when you ring the number quoted, there is resistance to you visiting the puppies in their home, forget it – don't go.

Do your homework

Research the breed thoroughly before you commit to a purchase. The Internet is a good source of information, as are the canine weekly newspapers. For useful addresses, contact numbers and websites of people who will help you find the right type of puppy, turn to page 126.

For Parson Russell Terriers, the Kennel Club will be your best source of information, followed by the breed clubs. To find breeders of the genuine working type of Jack Russell, contact

The puppies should not leave their mother and littermates to go to their new homes until they are at least eight weeks old.

the secretary of the regional section of the Jack Russell Club of GB. It would be a good idea to go to one of their shows where you can meet the breeders. Other good sources are places where dog owners congregate, such as training clubs. Veterinary surgeons can often help, too, as they will invariably know the local breeders. There are also Jack

Russells for rehoming in rescue centres, the best of which try to match the dogs with potential owners. Charities such as Dogs Trust and Battersea Dogs Home do their best to assess a dog's temperament and match him to a new home.

Viewing the puppies

Good breeders do not sell their puppies before they are at least eight weeks old, and, ideally, you should visit a litter when they are about six weeks old. This is a good opportunity to see the puppies with their mother in their own home. If you are looking for a family pet, take your children with you – these dogs are long lived and will be around for the children's formative years. Keep them

(the kids) under strict control, and remember that the puppies may never have seen small human beings before.

Ask to see the puppies' mother, and do not buy a pup if the breeder cannot or refuses to show her to you. You are looking for a well-balanced dog who has not got short piano legs with turned-out feet. This type of dog is probably a cross breed and, although it may be a good hunting dog, it will not be a real Jack Russell and the puppies will probably end up looking like their mother. Also, check the mother's temperament and how she responds to you; if she is fearful,

When you go to the breeder's to see the puppies, it is a good idea to examine them, checking their health and temperament.

cringes or is aggressive in any way, do not buy one of her puppies.

Likewise, take a crafty look around where the puppies are living. If their surroundings and bed are dirty or soiled and foul smelling, consider excusing yourself and just leave. Ideally, puppies should be raised in the breeder's own home – not an outhouse, barn, garage or outdoor kennels – in a clean, healthy environment where they can be well socialized and become accustomed to all the various household noises and the comings and goings of different people.

Examining the puppies

If you are satisfied that the puppies are of the type that you want and that their home environment is happy and healthy, study them closely. Watch how they play together and interact with their mother as well as their littermates. Try to gauge their temperament.

If you are looking for a bitch puppy, then ask the breeder to remove the dogs – or vice versa if you are looking for a male puppy. The most favoured colours most people look for in Jack Russells are completely white bodies with black and/or tan ears and round the eyes and a coloured patch at the root of the tail.

The puppy you are looking for should be a happy extrovert who is full of life, bold, unafraid and naturally curious. You should examine the puppy of your choice very carefully.

- Start off by checking that the puppy's upper and lower teeth are in line – the upper front teeth should be just over the lower in a scissor bite

- Make sure that the ears are clean and not smelly
- There must be no sign of mucus from the nose, vulva or rectum.

If you do decide to buy a puppy, the breeder may want to check on your credentials as a worthy potential owner, and you should not be offended if you are asked some pertinent or personal questions about your home, lifestyle and work. The breeder is not being nosy or prying into your affairs; they are protecting their puppy and ensuring that he goes to a good home where he will be loved and well looked after.

Agreement to purchase

The breeder may want you to leave a deposit to secure the puppy you like. By all means, leave a small one but get a written agreement that should the puppy not be in the same good condition in two weeks' time when he is ready to leave home, there is no contract to buy.

Some breeders, particularly those who register with the Kennel Club, may offer their buyers four to six weeks' free insurance and a 'buy back' agreement should the puppy not be suitable. Many people who breed the hunting-type Jack Russells are just as concerned about the future welfare of their puppies and they may offer similar facilities.

With either type, you must insist on getting a receipt for the money that you hand over and also ask for the puppy's papers. If they are not forthcoming, get an agreement that the breeder will apply for them and will send them to you in, say, two to three weeks.

Be prepared

Now is the time to prepare for the arrival of your new puppy. In the time between visiting him and making the decision to purchase and bring him home, there are certain preparations that you will need to make. Make sure that you have the following items of essential equipment before collecting the puppy:

- A crate which is big enough for the puppy when he is fully grown (this could be used for travelling, too)
- A bed – heavy plastic for preference (basketwork is ideal for chewing)

Crates are not cruel for puppies, although you should not leave them shut inside for too long. With some cosy bedding, toys and water, they can become a safe den for your dog.

- Vetbed or fleece bedding for comfort
- Two or three tough playthings and toys
- Two unchewable water and food dishes
- A light cat collar and lead
- A leather collar and lead to fit him when he is older
- An identification tag for the collar with your address and telephone number engraved on it
- A six- or eight-panel puppy play pen.

When I acquire a new puppy, I always prepare a cardboard box. I remove the top, cut a hole in the wall of the box which is big enough for a puppy to pass through, and then turn it upside down on a piece of Vetbed which I cover with a sweater from a member of the household. Puppies love to go inside; they get a sense of security and even if they chew it, it doesn't matter – I can always prepare another one.

Collecting your puppy

On the big day, don't go alone to pick up the puppy. Ideally, two people should collect him as he will need to be held and comforted in the car on the way home – he may never have been in a car before and nor will he have left his family. Take some towels and tissues with you in case he is travel sick.

Persuade the breeder to give you about seven days' worth of the food that the puppy is accustomed to eating – this will prevent stomach upsets in the transitory period. The breeder should also give you a diet sheet, detailing how often and when he should be fed.

If the puppy is old enough to have already had his first vaccinations, get the certificates to show your own vet. If he has not been vaccinated, do not let him out of the car to urinate in lay-bys under any circumstances – they are hotbeds of infection and it is not worth taking unnecessary risks.

A dog is at his most vulnerable regarding disease when he is a puppy or a pensioner, so, in view of the cost of a puppy and the high fees charged by vets, it is a good idea to purchase pet health insurance. Some breeders will even provide this, at least for a limited transitional period, and the Kennel Club makes arrangements when a puppy is transferred to the new owner.

Fortunately, the average Jack Russell is made of stern stuff and he will seldom

Other things to do

Find a vet you respect and like and tell him/her about your new addition. Make an appointment to see the vet two days after the puppy arrives home for a health check and to discuss his vaccinations.

Make certain that your garden really is escape proof. Jack Russells are notorious escapologists and the smallest hole attracts them like a bee to a flower. So check for any holes in fences, gaps in hedges, gates that can be crawled under, bars that are wide enough to allow a small puppy to squeeze through, and unprotected garden ponds.

Similarly, in the house, ensure that cupboard doors at ground level are securely closed, there are no trailing electrical leads or wires that can be chewed, and consider positioning a child gate at the bottom of steep stairs until the puppy is older and can go up and down safely.

need the attentions of the veterinary profession, but you never know what the future may bring – accidents can happen.

Coming home

The first thing to do when you arrive home is to take your new puppy out into the garden. When he performs (urinating or defecating), praise him lavishly. Whatever you do, however, you must not let the children go wild with him; he could get over-excited and leave an unpleasant deposit on your new carpet. He needs some quiet time to snuffle about and discover and get acquainted with his new surroundings.

Feeding your puppy

Give your puppy a small amount of food, make some fresh water available to him and call him by his name. Throw a little titbit into his box or basket to tempt him into it, but avoid feeding him sweets, cakes and chocolate, which is poisonous to dogs. Treats should consist of tiny morsels of cooked meat, liver or very small pieces of dog biscuit.

You should feed your puppy four small meals a day. His stomach is still very small, but as he grows the meals can get smaller in number but larger in quantity. By the time he is six to eight months, he can be fed just twice a day.

Initially, continue to give him the food recommended by the breeder, but you can gradually change it to whatever you have opted to use. However, don't do this too quickly, otherwise an upset stomach will ensue. Don't offer the puppy cow's milk unless his breeder has

Your puppy will need several small meals a day while he is still very young. Decrease the number gradually as he grows older.

given it to him from birth – some dogs find it difficult to digest. Your vet can supply you with a milk substitute which is adequate, if necessary. A dog can live a perfectly healthy life drinking only water.

Start training

It is never too early to start training and socializing your puppy, and there are some important things you need to start doing as soon as you bring him home. He will learn quickly and will soon get used to the new routine.

Using a crate

To get your puppy accustomed to going into his crate, simply feed him inside it. Give him the same command each time: 'In your box'. Leave the door open to start with as you want to get him used to going in and out without any stress. After about three days, shut him in for five to ten minutes and then gradually increase the length of time he is confined each day to about one hour. He will eventually travel happily in the crate or go in of his own accord for short periods of rest or sleep – the crate will become his den where he can escape from the busy world. Have it fitted with a water dispenser, but don't keep him confined for too long.

Using a puppy pen

You can also start to train him into his puppy pen; this will be a godsend when you want to vacuum the carpet – he'll probably want to kill the vacuum cleaner – or need to pop out to the shops for

half an hour. A puppy pen will keep him safe and secure. He can have his bed, toys and a water bowl inside, and watch everything that is going on around him without feeling isolated. Again, don't be too long or he will become anxious.

The first night

Before you put your puppy into his bed for the night, take him outside, wait for him to perform and then praise him enthusiastically. Spread sheets of clean newspaper all round the area where he sleeps. This is the beginning of house training, and the puppy will not want to soil his bedding. The first couple of

Your puppy will be safe in a puppy pen, which you can move around the house or garden. He can relax and watch the outside world.

nights are often quite difficult for both of you. Your puppy may squeak and howl with loneliness, and I am afraid that you must harden your heart because if you go to him he is, in effect, training you to come at his beck and call.

Some people go to the extent of sleeping in the same room as their new puppy for a few nights, but this is a bit extreme. As a last resort, you can take the puppy and his bed upstairs and place it beside your bed. If he becomes restless in the night, a hand on his head will comfort him. Don't, whatever you do, let him get into your bed – if you do, you will live to regret it, trust me.

The first few days
The first few days for a young puppy in his new home are of the ultimate importance. Puppies enjoy routine, so feed your dog at the same times, take him outside after every meal, drink and after any period of rest, and, above all, communicate and play with him.

On his first morning in your home, get up and greet your puppy happily, then put him outside and wait for him to perform, talking to him all the time.

Make sure that you go out with him, whatever the weather – don't just shove him out of the door and hope for the best. When he does his business, praise him lavishly and then give him his first meal of the day.

Microchipping and security
Now is also a good time to discuss microchipping with your vet. This involves a small electronic transponder being implanted painlessly between the puppy's shoulder blades. On it is recorded his number together with his owner's name and address, vet's details, the puppy's age, sex, etc., all of which can be read with a scanner.

The details will be logged with Petlog (see page 126), Britain's largest data base of dogs, which is used for the recovery of stolen or missing dogs. Jack Russells seem to be very attractive to dog thieves, and these devices are a deterrent. Many

Vaccinations
On the second day in his new home, take your puppy to the vet for a physical examination and to discuss his vaccinations. Don't take him into any public places for fear of infectious diseases until after the second vaccination. All mammals, including dogs, carry worms, and the vet will prescribe the appropriate tablets. The treatments should be carried out punctiliously. For more details on vaccinations and worming, see pages 103 and 105.

It is your responsibility as an owner to make sure that your puppy wears a collar to which an identity disc is attached with your details.

To comply with the law, all dogs should carry a name tag when out in a public place. This should be engraved with the name and address of the owner, but the dog's name should not appear. Many owners put a collar bearing a name tag on their dog in the morning and leave it on until the dog goes to bed. This can be a starting point should the dog get accidentally lost.

Simple obedience training

Whilst you are waiting for the time to pass before you can safely walk your puppy after his second vaccinations, you can begin a little simple training – nothing too taxing. Jack Russells have the reputation of being hyperactive and it is necessary to gain some control over your puppy right from the beginning of your relationship. Indeed, the earlier you start, the better it is. You can train him in short periods of between five and eight minutes, followed by a rest with some play. The two most used and important commands are 'Sit' and 'Come', so teach these first.

lost and stolen dogs have been found and returned to their owners as a result. A puppy can get lost simply because a door is left open; he is gone in a flash, disorientated and not knowing which way is home. Children and good-natured people, if you are lucky, may take him home with them and report their find to a dog warden. If so, he will apply his scanner and the puppy will be returned safely to you. The veterinary surgeon, too, will scan every new patient brought to him and can thus identify a lost dog.

An individual tattoo is an alternative, and the National Tattoo Register (see page 126) have qualified stock tattoo artists across the country. Each tattooed number, usually in the ear or the inside thigh, is unique to that puppy. Full details of the dog and his owner are registered which, again, makes it easy to reunite them if the dog gets lost.

Safety in the home

While your puppy is young, don't let him go up and down stairs – his bones are not yet fully developed, and if damage is done to the growth plates he will never be able to move accurately. A child's gate placed at the top and bottom of the stairs will solve the problem. If your dog must go upstairs with you, carry him.

Sit

Teaching your puppy to sit on command will be extremely useful. It will stop him jumping up at people, bothering you when you are busy or eating, and will generally help to make living together easier and more pleasurable.

Use food treats to get your puppy's attention initially and to reward him when he performs the desired action. He also needs lots of praise and fuss to show him that he has pleased you. With practice and patient repetition, he will soon learn to associate the word 'Sit' with the required action. Practise it often, in different places and situations, such as inside the house, in the garden and when crossing a road, but be sure to keep the training sessions short and fun, and always finish on a high note with a reward for success.

1 With your puppy on a lead, stand in front of him and attract his attention with a tasty treat.

2 When his eyes are focused on the hand holding the treat, raise it upwards and backwards just above his head.

3 As his head goes up to get the treat, his bottom should automatically go down and touch the ground.

4 When his bottom is on the ground in the sitting position, reward him instantly with the treat and praise him.

Come

Teaching a puppy to return to you on command is of paramount importance, so start training him from an early age. When your dog comes straight to you when you call him, always welcome him enthusiastically and reward him with a treat. If it helps, you can get down to his level with your arms outstretched. Practise this obedience training in the garden whenever your puppy goes out to relieve himself.

Training tip

Do the sequence once more and that will be enough for the first session. Repeat the exercise the next day and then do it once in the morning and again in the afternoon. Make it fun with little treats, and within a week your puppy will be coming to you happily on command.

I **Ask a friend to hold your puppy for you. Tell him firmly to 'Sit' and let him sniff your hand which should conceal a tasty treat.**

2 **Move slowly away from him, but still facing him, with your hand raised as shown. Your puppy should focus on the hand containing the treat.**

3 **A short distance away, squat down on the ground and call your puppy's name or give the command 'Come'.**

4 **Your friend can release the puppy and he should run towards you. Praise him lavishly and reward him with the treat.**

Alternative method

1 Using a small toy, such as a ball or whatever interests your puppy most, show it to him and get his attention.

2 Throw the toy a short distance, about 60cm (2ft), and encourage your puppy to go after it and pick it up.

3 When your puppy picks it up, call his name and add the word 'Come'. Get down on the ground at his level and encourage him to come back to you.

4 If he comes back to you immediately, reward him with a tasty treat and praise him enthusiastically. Play a game with him with the toy.

Lead training

Start lead training by putting a light cat collar round your puppy's neck and attaching a light lead to it. Let him run around the house and garden, trailing the lead until he gets used to it. Pick it up and gently influence the direction in which you want him to go. The idea is to prepare him mentally for what will happen when he starts walking on the lead properly after his vaccinations.

Exercise

Formal exercise is not required for a young puppy – a Jack Russell is so full of surplus energy that he is quite capable of giving himself sufficient exercise, particularly if he has a garden. However, when a puppy has had enough exercise and flops down for a rest, do not disturb him – just let him be and make sure the children allow him to sleep for as long as he wants. He should not be taken for long formal walks or allowed to play excessively until he is six months old. This will allow his joint growth plates to ossify. By all means, however, take him for short walks to familiarize him with the local area and get him used to traffic but not too much.

Socialization

This is the important process whereby you introduce your puppy to all aspects of life, including people, other dogs, all the different facets of household and family living, going out and about and experiencing a wide range of activities and social interaction. However, this has to be carried out on your terms with your dog under your control.

Attach a light lead to your puppy's collar and let him trail it behind him while moving about when you are outside in the garden.

In the home

Get your puppy accustomed to a wide range of household activities and noises, such as the television, washing machine, dishwasher, radio and vacuum cleaner. He will also need to meet as many different people as possible, including your friends and visitors, and all the tradespeople who come to your house.

Jack Russells are guard dogs by nature and they will warn of a visitor's approach by barking, and may even try to scare them off. Therefore you must introduce your puppy to the milkman, postman and bin men at a very early age.

If you already own other pets, you will have to introduce them to your

Your puppy will enjoy playing games with you. This is a useful way to exercise him physically and mentally as well as bonding.

puppy carefully, under close supervision. Never leave them alone together, even for short periods. Some Terrier puppies are more tolerant than others, but do remember that they are natural hunters, and pet rabbits, rats, hamsters, gerbils and guinea pigs are their natural prey. They will often end up befriending the family cat, but it may take time and patience, so don't try to rush the process. The younger your puppy is when he enters your household, the greater the chances of everyone living together peacefully in harmony.

In the outside world

As soon as you get the 'all clear' from your vet after his final vaccinations and can safely venture out with your dog, you can begin by taking him out for walks. Comfort him or pick him up to reassure him if any loud noise should frighten him. He will soon get used to

Socialize your puppy by taking him out for walks where he can experience traffic as well as meeting different people and other dogs.

traffic and huge, smelly, noisy vehicles passing within just a few feet of him.

Take your puppy to places where it is likely that there will be a lot of people – such as markets and train stations. Your dog must learn to avoid human feet, so that he does not get trodden on or trip people up. Let as many people as possible handle him, including friends, relations and even strangers.

Be a responsible owner

By law you are required to pick up your dog's mess in public places; failure to do so may result in a hefty fine. Be prepared and always carry plastic bags in your pocket should you have to scoop some up.

Never let your dog off the lead in a public place, no matter how well trained he is. He can be easily distracted, even by a piece of paper or a fluttering feather. If it's worth investigating or chasing, he will have a go and may disappear over the horizon in the process. Nor will he have any understanding of the potential dangers of traffic, and this will apply for the rest of his life. You can be absolutely sure that although your dog may do as he is told after many weeks of training, he is still likely to occasionally do the opposite, just for fun.

Clubs and classes

As soon as he is permitted to move outside, it's a good idea to take your puppy to a training club. Your vet can advise if there is one in your area. Indeed, some veterinary clinics run their own puppy training sessions. Most local canine clubs want to actively encourage puppy training and also run classes.

When your puppy attends, he will be taught how to behave in the company of other dogs as well as learning basic obedience and commands. This is good training for you, too. Why not take part in the Good Citizens Scheme, which was inaugurated by the Kennel Club to teach simple obedience? There is a system of awards, including Gold, Silver and Bronze. Children are usually very keen to join in and compete with their dogs for the medals and certificates. Training of this type will benefit all Jack Russells, whether they are destined to be family pets, working dogs or show dogs.

Government legislation

An increasing amount of legislation has been introduced concerning dogs and their owners. Some of these laws are draconian with the punishments out of proportion to the 'crime'. The Dangerous Dogs Act 1991 is a case in point. If your Jack Russell quarrels with another dog in the park and bites it, a complaint made may result in a court case with dire consequences for your dog. If your dog goes for a cat, the same thing may happen. The central issue will be that your dog is out of control, so it behoves you not to let this happen and to make every effort to ensure that he is well behaved and under your control at all times. Good socialization and training from an early age will prevent future behaviour problems and help you to bond with your dog. They are the foundations for a long and happy relationship.

Chapter 3

The adult dog

By the time your pet Jack Russell reaches adulthood – usually at around one year old – he should be well behaved and under your control. However, you will have discovered by now that your Terrier has an independent nature, and although he may obey you, the person who trains him, he may ignore everyone else.

He will be feisty where it matters and affectionate to his family to an extraordinary degree. This is a highly intelligent breed, and you will find that your dog will understand your body language and rapidly attune to your moods. Of course, like any other breed, there will be variations in character, and some dogs are quieter by nature than others, depending on early socialization together with genetic influences.

Rehoming an adult dog

If you do not want to have the trouble of bringing up a puppy, you might consider rehoming an adult dog. Such dogs occasionally become available for various reasons, such as the death of an owner, divorce and family breakdown, or owners moving abroad. To start your search, telephone either the secretary of the Jack Russell Club of Great Britain or the Parson Russell Terrier Club (see page 126). They should be able to put you in touch with a breed rescue in your area. The rescue staff will probably know a little of the dog's history and training and can brief you accordingly. Of course, some of these dogs are house-trained and quite well behaved, while others, especially in bigger sanctuaries that cater for all breeds, may have been abandoned or are strays with no training or social graces. If you decide to take on such a dog, you must be patient and prepared to spend a lot of time training, working and playing with him to win his trust and build up a rewarding relationship.

A Jack Russell Terrier is not the right dog for everyone; some people find them too energetic and independent, and they really need an active family. Most rescue centres try to match dogs to potential owners and have a relatively good idea of what works. As a potential owner, you will be interviewed and asked some searching questions. For example, they

Opposite: The adult Jack Russell is alert, inquisitive and full of fun, always ready for work or a game or a walk. These dogs love human company and like to feel valued members of their family 'pack'.

may want to know whether your garden is escape-proof, if you work or whether there will be someone at home during the day, and the ages of your children in order to satisfy themselves that your home is suitable. Some even carry out a home visit just to check the facilities. There is no need to feel offended by these checks; the rescue centres are bound by law to satisfy themselves that the welfare of the dog is not in jeopardy. There is usually a small donation to pay before the dog is released into your care.

The genuine article

There is a problem associated with acquiring a Jack Russell from these sources, and it is a question of identity. How will you know that the dog is a genuine Jack and not a strange mixture masquerading as one? Make no mistake: he may be a perfectly good little dog, but he may not be a real Jack Russell. If you have friends who know their Terriers, take them along to see the dog you are thinking of adopting. Otherwise, study the Standards (see pages 20 and 22) and remember that the genuine article:

• Has folded ears
• Will weigh between 6–8kg (13–18lb)
• Is basically white with black or black and tan patches on his head and, hopefully, a patch at the root of his tail
• Will not have short, bowed legs – they will be in proportion to his body.

Be patient

You will soon have a good idea of your new dog's nature and the depth of his training. It's possible that he'll need lots of tender loving care and understanding to undo any faults and behaviour problems that may have become embedded. Above all, be patient but persistent. Never, ever show anger or shout at your dog because this is counter productive. Jack Russells have a good memory and may well become resentful and mutinous.

Now is the time to bond with him, play with him and talk to him. Always use his name and do not be harsh, even if he does something wrong. Also, make sure you feed him in the same place at the same time each day. If he is fully vaccinated and lead trained, take him for walks at least twice a day, so that he learns where he is and how to find his way home. Remember that he must wear an ID tag all the time he is out – get one made and attach it to his collar.

Take your puppy to training classes, so that he will learn to behave with other dogs and strangers. Here, you can both enrol for the Kennel Club's Good Citizens Scheme and learn some simple obedience. Full details of the Scheme and its awards can be found later on in Chapter 4 (see page 76).

Neutered dogs

Many dogs and bitches from rescue centres are neutered. This is because there is a strong moral argument not to allow unplanned pregnancies. Jack Russells are escapologists – they can squeeze through the smallest holes and scale high fences – so many end up as strays in rescue centres. You may also wish to consider getting your own dog neutered. If your bitch is on heat and

unable to resist the call of nature to mate, she might escape and get mated by the local wandering Collie. Alternatively, your male dog may get the scent of a bitch in season and mate the mini Dachshund up the road whose owner will not be happy.

Therefore if you do not intend to let your bitch have puppies, you should have her spayed. Not only will you not

Jack Russells are game little dogs and make great companions, especially if you work them or enjoy participating in activities such as Terrier racing, Agility or Flyball.

have the aggravation of unwanted puppies but also you will not have the nuisance of confining the bitch for three weeks every six months or so when she comes into season. Castrating a dog should stop him leaving home when

he scents a bitch in season, which he can do up to two miles away. If an entire dog cannot get to the bitch he scents, he may fret and even lose weight. Some people say that a neutered dog will gain weight, but if they get proper exercise and a balanced, controlled diet this should not happen. There is evidence that the coat texture can change, however, and become more abundant after neutering.

Older dogs from breeders

The other source of older dogs that you may wish to consider is breeders who sometimes keep dogs and bitches for potential breeding and/or show stock. If, for some reason, they do not come up to the standard expected, e.g. the set or size of their ears may be wrong or perhaps their tail is set too far over the back, they may want to rehome them. However, this will not have any effect on their pet or even working quality. Dogs who have spent their lives in kennels often make extremely good pets;

A rescue dog needs lots of your attention, companionship and understanding as well as exercise and opportunities for free running.

they seem to appreciate the comfort that comes from contact with humans. However, remember that many kennel dogs have had little if any training for most domestic situations, so you will be starting from scratch. If the dog is an ex-show dog, he will be used to travelling in a box, walking on a lead under control round the show ground, performing in the ring and ignoring other dogs.

Feeding your dog

After play, exercise and work, a dog's main interest in life is eating. Whether it is better to feed once or twice a day has long been the subject of argument. Many well-known breeders feed their dogs twice a day – a small amount in the morning and a larger meal in the evening. This is because a fed dog is quieter and more restful at night after a meal and livelier during the day as a result of a small breakfast. If you want the opposite, a watchful dog at night, you just reverse the procedure.

Which food is best?

Whether to feed a complete diet or a mixed natural diet has been debated since commercial foods became available. Some breeders do not believe that their dogs thrive on the same commercially prepared food fed on a daily basis, and think that staying alive and thriving are totally different things. In the natural state, the dog is an omnivore, eating meat and vegetable-based substances. Wild dogs catch their prey and eat the stomach contents first. The prey is usually a herbivore, so this is vegetation. Next, they eat the internal organs and, lastly, the muscle meat. This is mentioned to illustrate the diverse dietary requirements of canines in their wild state.

Dogs derive a sensory pleasure from biting into a juicy piece of meat, so why deprive them of it? There is, however, no denying that prepared complete diets are very convenient for owners with busy lives, although, in my opinion, they are not always the best way of feeding your pet. A dog is a creature of habit, so it is best to feed him at approximately the same time(s) every day. No matter what is fed, there should always be a copious amount of fresh, clean water available.

How much protein?

It is popularly thought that the more protein ingested by a dog, the better. Not true – the correct amount of protein is in direct proportion to the amount of activity. Dogs that habitually have more

Adult Jack Russells love their food and it is very important to feed them a nutritious, well-balanced diet to keep them healthy.

protein than is necessary can often suffer from skin and coat disorders. If your Terrier is out all day hunting rats, he will need a diet with a higher protein and calorie content than a sedentary pet dog. However, if you go on a walking holiday with your dog, he will need an increase in protein and calories. As a pet owner, you will be astonished at the amount of energy a Jack Russell has and the distances that he can run.

Ask your vet about which foods to feed your dog and how much and how often, if you are not sure whether you are doing it right. Be careful not to overdo the supplements if you prepare your own food. Complete diets should not need the addition of supplements as they are added during manufacture.

Canned food

For pet owners with one or two dogs, canned food is a convenient way to feed them, although it does vary in cost and content. The average moisture content of the best is about 25 per cent, whereas the cheapest can be as much as 75 per cent. It usually consists of meat, offal and tripe with some vegetables and gravy or jelly in different proportions. The protein and calorific content is usually written on the label on the can, and half a can of the best quality with a handful of mixer or ordinary dog biscuit will be adequate for the average pet Jack Russell.

Pouches and frozen food

Pet food in pouches is 'semi moist' and contains around 25 per cent moisture. Meat based, it invariably contains

Special diets

If your dog suffers from a digestive problem or has an upset tummy, your vet may recommend a special diet for him, such as chicken and rice. Some companies even make special foods for delicate stomachs, and these are often available from veterinary surgeries.

Likewise, if you suspect that your dog may have an allergy, do consult your vet for advice. Allergies can be quite hard to manage, and it is often difficult to ascertain the cause.

preservatives and, like canned food, it can be offered to your dog either with biscuit or a mixer. Frozen dog food, which is delivered right to your door, is rapidly becoming increasingly popular due to its convenience. This consists of quality meat with no additives, but it is not available in all areas.

Fresh food

Preparing fresh food for your dog takes very little time, and you can feed him chopped meat (after removing any bones), offal, chicken or fish. If using fish, do be sure to check carefully for bones as these can easily get stuck in a dog's throat and can be very dangerous. Add some vegetables, such as chopped carrots, cabbage and peas, and a handful of biscuit and serve in the cooking liquid. You can also try adding pasta, rice or even some table scraps and leftovers, but not potatoes or onions.

Keeping slim and fit

A dog is a running machine and he should not be permitted to become overweight. As in humans, obesity is an increasing problem among dogs and a risk to their health and longevity. It is your duty, as a responsible owner, to find out from the breeder or your vet what your dog should weigh and to monitor his weight and fitness. If your dog is overweight, take him for three or four short walks every day and gradually increase them in length and duration, but without exhausting him. Cut out all treats, except small pieces of cooked liver for training purposes, and never feed him sweets, biscuits and cakes.

Jack Russells are active dogs and they need daily walking on a lead and free running.

Exercising your dog

The Jack Russell is the all-action dog and it is almost impossible to wear him out with ordinary exercise. If you live in a town, two good walks a day will probably suffice but they should be augmented with play in the garden, chasing and retrieving a ball or playing with a Frisbee. All these games and activities contribute to your dog's physical fitness and mental stimulation. Free running is very important but always ensure that your dog is strictly under control – he must not be loose near a busy road as he will have no real sense of the danger of traffic. If you are worried about this, exercise him on a long retractable lead. In the country, he can run free in fields where there is no livestock, but be careful as farmers are

legally entitled to shoot dogs that chase and worry their cows or sheep. Lastly, keep your dog well away from badger setts, rabbit holes and fox earths as most Jacks will go to ground and you may have problems digging your dog out.

Perhaps one of the most exciting ways to exercise your dog is to join a club that teaches Agility and Flyball. Both these sports demand a lot of energy, and you and your dog will enjoy participating.

Grooming

Jack Russells of both varieties come in several coats. The KC Standard for the Parson Russell Terrier asks for a

Use your time together when out on walks and playing games to bond with each other and build a mutually rewarding relationship.

rough or smooth coat, both of which should be close and dense.

Grooming the smooth coat

This is the easiest coat to deal with as it only requires a weekly brush and perhaps a finishing polish with a hound glove. The exception is during the moulting period when frequent brushing will get rid of the shedding hairs, making room for new growth. It is better for the hairs to end up on a brush rather than on your best sofa and carpets.

Grooming the rough coat

In practice, the rough coat is a wire-type coat which does not moult, but it does need a brush and comb about twice a week. As it grows longer, however, it will tangle and collect detritus from the undergrowth, making regular grooming particularly important for working dogs. The long hairs of pets also need tidying to keep them looking smart, and this is best done with the dog on a table. Start by plucking the hairs out by hand – this is easy if the hair is long and ready. Although it does not hurt the dog, he may get irritated to start with if he has

It is easier to pluck out the hairs between your forefinger and thumb if you wear rubbers on them. Just pull them out gently; it won't hurt your dog and he'll get used to it.

A smooth-coated Jack Russell only requires a quick groom with a slicker or hound glove. It glides through the coat, massaging the skin.

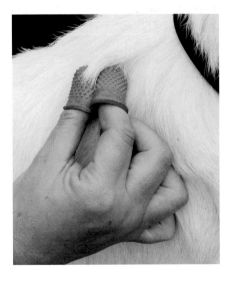

to stand still for too long. If you are removing the hair from around the shoulders (the mantle), grasp the skin between your finger and thumb in the area and, with the finger and thumb of the other hand, gently pull half a dozen hairs out. You can buy special stripping knives to speed up the process.

Work your way all over the dog but stop if he gets restive. It may be necessary for a second person to hold his head – a hand on either side of it will prevent him from biting. Don't stress the dog for too long; little but often is the answer in the early days. Eventually he'll get used to it and will tolerate it for fairly long periods.

Note: If you cut the hair with scissors you alter the texture, making it softer and, in the case of a dog with colour, you may dilute the colour.

Grooming the broken-haired coat

The Jack Russell Club of Great Britain's Standard asks for a smooth, rough or broken-haired coat. The broken-haired coat is quite different from the smooth or rough varieties:

- It is slightly softer to the touch and grows longer if left
- It does not moult significantly
- The long hairs should be plucked in a similar way to the rough coat (see page 55).

Note that although this type of coat will not find favour among the judges of a Kennel Club beauty show, it will be acceptable, however, at a JRC show because their judges' priority is function.

Use a stripping comb on rough and broken-haired coats, working your way along the dog's back from the neck to the hindlegs.

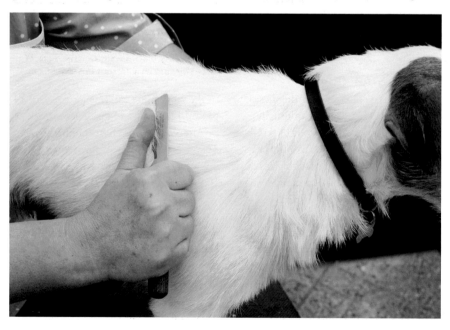

Checking your dog

Grooming is the ideal time to check your dog over and make sure there are no telltale signs of forthcoming health problems. Start by parting his coat and looking for fleas. Their presence can be detected by tiny black specks, about the size of a pin head. If you discover some, dust the dog with flea powder or some other treatment (ask your vet or see page 104) and wash his bedding.

You may even spot a tick in your dog's skin, especially if he exercises out in fields where livestock are kept. For advice on removing them, see page 105.

Look inside your dog's ears and check for any signs of infection or a build up of wax, and also check his eyes – there should be no discharge. This is a good opportunity to clean his teeth, and you can now buy special dog toothbrushes and toothpaste. It is easier to get him accustomed to being handled in this way if you start while he is still a puppy.

Use your grooming sessions to check your dog all over for signs of ill health or parasites. Carefully part his coat and look for the telltale sooty black specks that are signs of fleas. They are easy to spot in a white coat.

Bathing your dog

Whichever type of coat your dog has, it will not retain dirt, and it can usually be brushed out. However, if your dog rolls in something particularly noxious, he may need a bath. It will probably take two people to bath him – one to hold and the other to wash him – and you must both be prepared to get really wet.

Before you start bathing him, smear a little petroleum jelly around his eyes, and then stand him in a sink or bath with tepid water up to the level of his stomach. Using a special dog shampoo, lather his coat, paying special attention to the rectum area and being very careful to avoid his eyes and inside his ears.

Afterwards, rinse him thoroughly to remove all the traces of the shampoo. You can rough dry him with a towel. If it's a hot, sunny day, you can even let your dog run around outside and dry off naturally, but otherwise you may wish to use a hairdryer on the warm setting, being careful not to burn him. Some Jack Russells do not like this and are nervous of the noise of the hairdryer, so, if this is the case, be patient and reassure him while you dry him off.

Dog theft

Jacks Russells are very vulnerable to being stolen. It is a sad fact that thousands of dogs of all breeds are stolen every year, and thieves want Jacks for illegal badger baiting, dog fighting and other nefarious activities. The unbendable rules are as follows:

1 Never leave your dog alone in an unlocked car – no dog should be left in a car anyway on a sunny, warm day, as they easily overheat and could die before help arrives.

2 Never leave your dog tied up outside a shop or in any public place.

3 Never leave your dog unattended in your garden if there is easy access to a lane or the gate is unlocked. It would be wise to invest in a high fence and to put a strong padlock and chain on the gate, especially if your garden is not overlooked and thieves can do their work unobserved.

Should the unthinkable happen
- Waste no time in reporting the theft to the police and insist on them giving you a crime number
- If your dog has been microchipped, report the loss to Petlog (see page 126) and then phone every vet and animal sanctuary in the surrounding area of about 10 square miles
- Contact the dog wardens in your county as well as surrounding ones
- Get your local paper, radio and television stations to feature your loss – if you have a photo of your dog, it will make it more interesting
- If you have access to a computer, make a poster with a photo of the dog and get it displayed in all the local shops, including newsagents and pet shops
- There are two organizations on the Internet that specialize in helping people whose dogs have been stolen or missing (see page 126). Check out these sites
- Lastly, don't ever give up hope. Many dogs have been found and returned to their owners even after several years, simply because they have been identified by their microchip or tattoo.

Be responsible as an owner and never take risks that may lead to your dog being stolen.

Travel

When travelling with your dog, always bear in mind Rule No 1, which should never be broken: never leave a dog in a car in the sun, as even with the windows slightly open the interior can heat up dramatically. On an average summer's day with an outside temperature of 25°C (75°F) the interior can reach up to 50°C (120°F) in dark-coloured cars which will literally cook the dog alive! Remember that a small Terrier can escape through a window left open just 10cm (4in).

Dogs are similar to humans when they travel – some are travel sick, and some are not. If your dog has been trained to go into a box or cage since he was a puppy you are less likely to have problems. Pop him into a cage in the back of the car and take him for a short ride. If, after five to ten miles, he settles down, he is unlikely to be ill on a longer run. When you get home, play a little game, give him a treat and let him think going out in the car is fun.

Travelling crates

Some people claim that putting a dog into a crate is cruel, but if he is trained this is absolute rubbish! Dogs like it – they have a sense of security and are not thrown about by any sudden movement of the car. It makes sense to travel with your dog confined in a box or crate.

Custom-made travelling boxes and crates are available from good pet shops. They should have plenty of ventilation and a door that is easily opened from outside. A dog should be able to stand with a space of 5–7.5cm (2–3in) above

Your dog will be more secure travelling in a crate in the back of your car. Make it cosy for him with a blanket and some toys.

his head, and lie down at full stretch. Put a piece of Vetbed or blanket on the floor of the crate and carry a spare one in case the original gets soiled.

You can buy special bottles for water, which clip on inside the crate, and even battery-driven fans affixed to the wire door. With all the glass in a modern five-door car, heat can be generated even when moving, so if your car is equipped with air-conditioning, use it.

The crate should be secured firmly onto the car's safety belt system. Special dog harnesses are also available which clip onto a safety belt. We have all seen TV pictures of a puppet child being thrown through the windscreen after a sudden stop, and the same would happen to a dog with the attendant risk of him injuring the people sitting in the front. The back door of a car could be flung open in an accident, and if this happens your dog would escape onto the road if he was not confined. Some dogs are so frightened by the experience that they run off and are never seen again, so don't let this happen to you.

If you want to take your dog abroad on holiday, you must get him a Pet Passport.

Dealing with travel sickness

If you have the misfortune of owning a travel-sick dog, do not give him tablets designed specifically for human beings. Instead, get suitable tablets from your vet. There appear to be two types of canine travel sickness. The first – and the easiest to deal with – is when the dog vomits the entire contents of his stomach in one or two convulsions.

If this happens, clean him up and make sure he drinks some water to prevent dehydration. Most dogs suffering this type of sickness recover very quickly.

The second type is when the dog salivates and can do so for several hours. This makes everything surrounding him, including his coat, sticky and messy. He becomes dehydrated rapidly and is miserable. If your dog is affected, keep plenty of water on hand. It is thought that this may be psychosomatic: the dog expects it to happen each time he gets into a car, so it is difficult to break the habit. If this is the case, consult your vet who may prescribe a very mild sedative, and when the dog finds that he's not sick it should not happen again. The sedative must be mild, as you do not want your dog half asleep in the show ring or when he is out working.

Pet Passport Scheme

Since 2000, it has been possible for dogs to enter the UK without going into quarantine but only through designated, specified sea and air ports and provided that the countries from which they are travelling are those with a reciprocal agreement (e.g. EU countries). There are other countries from which dogs can be imported into the UK without being quarantined, so visit the DEFRA website for more information (see page 126). If you intend to travel abroad to the designated countries with your dog and to return to the UK, you will need a Pet Passport. To get this, you must start the procedure with your vet about eight months before your intended journey.

What to do

It is important that the regulations are carried out in the correct order. First, have your pet tattooed by the National Tattoo Register, then microchipped by the vet before his rabies vaccination. The following details must be recorded:
- Your dog's birth date and age
- Microchip number, insertion date and location
- The date of the vaccination
- The vaccine manufacturer, product name and batch number
- The date by which the first booster vaccination must be given, i.e. 'valid until' date, calculated by reference to the validity period of the vaccine.

The vet should read the chip each time you visit in order to ensure that it still works and has not moved.

Your dog will be blood tested about 30 days after the vaccination to confirm that it has 'taken', and a waiting period of six months begins before he can be brought back into the country. When all the regulations have been met, a pet passport will be issued by the Local Veterinary Inspector (LVI). You will now be in a position to take your dog on holiday and bring him back into the UK with the following provisos:
- He must be treated against ticks and tapeworms by a vet not less than 24 hours and not more than 48 hours before the return journey
- His microchip number must be recorded on the veterinary certificate of treatment
- The product used for the tapeworm treatment must contain 'praziquantel'.

Right from the start, you need to know which regulations apply when travelling through other countries en route as well as in your country of destination – veterinary requirements differ. Telephone the nearest DEFRA office (see page 126) for the latest information. Your vet will see to it that your dog meets the criteria.

Mediterranean countries

If travelling to Mediterranean countries, be aware of canine Leishmaniasis (CanL), a severe disease of dogs which can, rarely, be passed on to humans. From 2000 to 2007, over 114,500 dogs utilizing the Pets Passport Scheme (PPS) have entered the UK, many of whom were returning holidaymakers from the warm countries bordering the Mediterranean. During that period, 690 dogs were diagnosed as having CanL. Because of the difficulty in diagnosing this disease it is estimated

that the same number have it without being diagnosed. It behoves every owner to take some easy, preventative steps.

The parasite is carried by a sandfly, which looks like a mini mosquito, but the name is a misnomer, as it does not live on beaches but in parks and woods. Its breeding season is around six months, starting in May. The female fly, feeding at dusk and dawn, takes a blood meal from the dog while depositing parasites in his skin. They enter the dog's blood stream, then the cells and eventually invade the internal organs. CanL in dogs cannot be cured but it can be controlled with expensive drugs. Only a blood test will confirm the disease.

What you can do

- Bring your dog indoors just before dusk and keep him there until dawn
- Spray the room in which he sleeps with insecticide
- Buy a Scalibor Protective band (collar) and keep it on your dog for 24 hours every day, starting two weeks before you travel and finishing the day after you leave. These special collars are impregnated with a chemical that either kills the fly or disorientates it to such a degree that it cannot bite. Available only from vets, they have an effective life of six months and are impervious to water. As a bonus, they are also very effective against ticks.

A word of warning

The documentation regarding the Pet Passport must be in order; if it is not, the authorities will condemn your dog to six months' quarantine at your expense. Here is a useful tip derived from my own experience: buy your own scanner and keep it with you throughout your holiday. Note that while every effort has been made regarding the accuracy of this information, potential travellers should also consult their vet and/or check the DEFRA website.

Opposite: When travelling with your dog, whether it is in Britain or on the Continent, be aware of potential disease and dangers, and take preventative action.

Chapter 4

Behaviour and training

In recent years, the process of dog training has become almost scientific. Animal behaviour is now studied formally, particularly that of dogs. In the UK, it is embedded in law that a dog in a public place must always be under the control of his owner. In this chapter, two modern training methods are examined, which, if taken to their conclusions, will bring any dog to a high standard of obedience.

Breed characteristics

Probably the best description ever of the breed is to be found on the website Jack Russells Online: 'First and unequivocally, foremost, the Jack Russell is a hunting Terrier! Anyone who thinks this incredible, energetic, highly intelligent, incurably curious bundle of iron muscles whose actions are directed by steel springs will be anything but miserable trying to live a sedate life in city or suburb is in for a tragic surprise. These fellows are often described as being 150 pounds of dog in a 10 pound body and no truer words have been spoken'.

Every dog breed has a different learning capacity, temperament and behavioural pattern, and each puppy within the breed is different from another.

The Jack Russell is a breed of high intelligence as well as being incredibly volatile, which, when combined with extreme bravery, makes him unique and difficult to mould. Most Jack Russell puppies have a similar nature, to a greater or lesser degree, which means they are not the easiest dogs to manage. Behaviourists cannot teach owners persistence and patience, but if you exercise these two traits when training your Jack Russell, you will succeed.

Typical behaviour

It is difficult to describe the behaviour of a typical Jack Russell, whether he is a KC registered Parson Russell Terrier or a JRCGB Hunt Jack Russell, simply because he is an individual and is also extremely self willed. If he thinks that he can get away with something, he will do what he pleases. One of the most

Opposite: Being alert and intelligent dogs, Jack Russells are easily trained if you are patient and make the sessions fun.

endearing characteristics of this breed is their playfulness. Inventive and mischievous, they enjoy one-to-one play. Hunting for a ball in long grass and bushes is a natural extension of their hunting instincts; retrieving sticks and balls is fun; and a game with a Frisbee is even better. Playing with your dog is a form of communication, reinforcing the bonding process and giving you more control, while providing your Jack Russell with the mental stimulation that is so necessary for Terriers.

Jack Russells like nothing better than to be off the lead outside in the country, scenting and hunting for potential prey.

The hunting instinct

Whether they can live happily in a city or suburb is open to argument – Jack Russells are a very flexible breed and they will adjust readily to any lifestyle that provides them with plenty of exercise, mental stimulation and human understanding. However, at heart, they are essentially working country dogs, and they love to be out in the open air. Even if they are cosseted city pets, their minds will be seldom far away from hunting, and they will still scour the garden, searching the undergrowth and bushes in their quest for moles, squirrels, mice or rats right into old age.

Genetic inheritance

Naturally some Jack Russells are keener on hunting than others – the genes controlling hunting will be polygenic and complex and they will depend on which ones they inherit from the sire and dam. If a puppy receives a potent hunting gene from both parents he will be a hot hunter, while another puppy in the same litter may receive a different set of hunting genes which could cause his attitude to be different.

It is easy to see that if a breeder's main priority is to maintain or improve the hunting qualities of their stock, they will breed known good hunters together. This system is known as selective breeding. Breeders whose priority is perceived beauty may dilute the hunting instinct to a certain degree in their own strain of dogs after several generations. This does not mean that their dogs will not hunt, but there is a possibility that they may not be quite so enthusiastic, although some may still be dealt a mixture of potent hunting genes. No-one can be sure what the genetic make-up will be – that is one of the fascinations of dog breeding.

Training your dog

Jack Russells have a reputation for being wild and virtually untrainable, but this is mainly because many inexperienced owners do not know how to control them. An extremely intelligent dog, a Jack is very perceptive and can learn quite complicated tasks if he has respect for the person who is teaching him. This is gained by patient, firm and kind teaching – exhibiting anger is always counterproductive when training dogs.

Jack Russells, whether they are hunting dogs or pet dogs, need a certain amount of training or they drive their owners mad with their high-velocity living. By teaching your dog basic obedience as a puppy, so he can sit, stay and come to you on command, he will be better behaved as an adult and less likely to argue or fight with other dogs. As a bonus, he will be more receptive to further training. Ideally, you should spend some time with him every day – in short bursts – reinforcing the basic commands: 'Sit', 'Stay' and 'Come'. We have already covered 'Sit' (see page 39) and 'Come' (see page 40) in basic training for young puppies. Now is the time to build on this foundation and introduce some new commands.

Small pets

Be warned: if your children own small furry animals as pets, e.g. rabbits or hamsters, they will be in imminent danger if you take on an adult Jack Russell. If your Jack is only eight or nine weeks old and you carefully introduce him to the small pet under strict supervision there should be no trouble. They will need to meet under controlled circumstances two or three times a day for at least a week, but even so there are no guarantees that this will be successful.

'Heel'

A well-behaved Jack Russell should always walk quietly at your side on a loose lead, without pulling too far forwards or deviating backwards or from side to side. No responsible dog owner should allow their dog to walk without any lead control on any type of road, however quiet they may seem.

Therefore it is essential that you train your puppy from the earliest possible age to walk happily on a lead at your side. If your dog is a pleasure to walk, you will both enjoy going out together. However, if he pulls you along or drags behind you, walks will become a battle ground instead of a fun experience.

1 Start off by holding the lead in your right hand across your body, with your dog standing on your left side. Lure him into position with a tasty treat.

2 Encourage him to move forwards at a normal pace, and then praise him enthusiastically and give him the treat when he starts trotting beside you.

Introducing a verbal command

When you have taught your dog to focus on walking correctly by your side, you can introduce a vocal command in order to remind him to do so and reinforce the training, such as 'Heel'. He will soon learn to associate the required action with the verbal command you use.

Rewards

When your dog behaves well and does what you ask, reward his good behaviour with praise, a stroke and a treat. This will reinforce what he has learnt and encourage him to please you and obey your commands.

3 Keep checking the lead. If it goes tight or the dog stops, pulls backwards or forwards, or goes in another direction, stop walking. Ask him to 'Sit' beside you.

4 Praise him when he sits in position, reward him with a titbit and then start walking again. Offer him little treats as you go along to reward good behaviour.

'Stay'

You should have already taught your puppy to 'Sit' (see page 39). When he has learnt this and will go into the position on command, you can progress by teaching him to 'Stay'. He may find this quite difficult at first as his natural instinct is to be with you, his owner, and you are going to ask him to remain at a distance from you. If wished, you can put a collar and extending lead on him when teaching this command, so that you have some control over him. After some patient practice sessions, he will gradually learn what is required and you will be able to move a little further away, increasing the distance between you.

Training tips

1 Never leave your dog just sitting in the 'Stay' for long periods. He may get bored and eventually wander off or even bolt.

2 Have a release word that you always use to break the 'Stay', such as 'Come' or just call him to you by his name.

3 You can progress gradually with this exercise until your dog will stay sitting for 15–20 minutes, or even when you go out of sight.

1 Begin with your dog in the 'Sit' position in front of you. Hold up your hand, with the flat of your hand towards him, and tell him firmly to 'Stay'.

2 If your dog stays in the same position and does not try to move, make sure that you praise him well and reward him with a tasty treat.

3 When your dog gets used to staying in the 'Stay' position for a few minutes without moving, you can move a few paces away from him, giving the hand signal and command. Be sure to keep eye contact with him.

4 After a few minutes, break the 'Stay' by calling your dog to you and, again, rewarding him when he comes to you with a treat and plenty of praise.

'Down'

This is a very useful command to teach, especially to Jack Russells who have a natural predisposition to jumping up at people to greet them. As with the other commands you teach your dog, it is very important to limit the words that you use and always to employ the same ones in order to avoid any confusion. Teach your family to use the same words as you. It is useful to teach this exercise in a range of different places and situations with varying degrees of distraction going on around you, so your dog does not associate it with just one location. Use the command when putting your dog to bed or meeting other dogs on a walk.

1 Ask your dog to 'Sit' in front of you, holding a tasty treat in your hand just above his head.

2 Gradually lower the hand holding the reward between his legs, but keeping it within his field of vision.

3 As you lower your hand on to the ground, say 'Down'. Your dog should move his front legs forward as he follows the treat until his elbows touch the ground and he lies down to get it.

4 Praise your dog and make a fuss of him immediately when he lies down and give him the treat to reward his good behaviour. Keep practising this until he will lie down on command.

'Fetch'

You can start playing retrieving games with your puppy as soon as you bring him home. At first he may run off with the toy or ball you throw for him but eventually he will learn to bring it back to you on command. This has many benefits, as retrieving games are fun as well as being extremely good exercise for an energetic Jack Russell. As always, keep the training sessions short and be patient with your dog, as it may take some time for him to master what you are teaching. Terriers are not natural retrievers, but they can be taught to bring things back for you if they are rewarded with treats and games.

I Show your dog a really interesting lightweight toy which he can easily pick up and carry. Wave it around and get him interested in it.

2 When you have his attention, throw the toy a short distance. Give the command 'Fetch' and encourage him to chase after it and pick it up.

3 When he picks it up, praise him well and call him to you. Run backwards to tempt him to follow you, saying 'Come'.

4 Don't grab the toy out of his mouth. Praise and stroke him and offer him a treat before gently taking it from him.

'Drop'

The Jack Russell has a very annoying habit of picking up all manner of rubbish, bits of paper, plastic, stones, and if you chase your dog and try to force him to surrender what he has in his mouth, he is likely to swallow it. This habit can cost you a lot of money at the veterinary surgery.

However, it is possible to train your dog to drop the things he holds in his mouth – dangerous or unpleasant ones as well as toys or your favourite shoes. It is best to start doing this while he is a puppy and before his teeth get big. Always praise him enthusiastically for coming back to you and reward him when he complies.

1 Ask your dog to 'Sit' (see page 39) when he has something in his mouth.
2 Praise him lavishly when he does so, and then put your hand on the object and say 'Drop'.
3 As he opens his mouth to let you remove the object, give him a small treat and praise him. He will soon learn that it is worth his while to relinquish the object to get the treat.

'Leave it'

Another important task for your dog is to learn to leave an object alone on your command. This behaviour is best learnt during puppyhood, starting with the removal of his food for a few moments accompanied by the words 'Leave it'. When he gives up his food, reward him with an immediate treat and some praise. Carry on this training with his treats, and soon he will associate the command word with anything he wants to pick up, including toys, other dog's faeces, etc.

Practise removing your dog's food bowl occasionally for a few minutes when he is eating and saying 'Leave it' as you do so.

'Wait'

When your dog has learnt to sit and stay on command, it is time to train him not to pass through doors – house doors or car doors – before you do. This is taught to prevent him dashing out into traffic from your front door, garden gate or car.

In fact, it may be a good idea to fix some heavy-duty return springs on the doors to prevent any mishaps occurring.

This is easy to teach when your dog has mastered the commands 'Sit' and 'Stay'. Sit your dog by the door and tell him to 'Stay'. Open the door. Your dog's impulse will be to rush through it, but tell him to 'Sit' and 'Stay' again. You must be prepared to close the door in his face if he tries to go through. It will only be necessary to do this a few times before he realizes that he cannot pass.

When you can open the door without the dog moving, you go through slowly, repeating the commands 'Sit' and 'Stay'. When you have succeeded in going through without the dog moving, give him the command 'Come'.

You can train your dog to wait for you to pass through gates and doors ahead of him. This will help to keep him safe and avoid situations that could lead to accidents.

Clicker training

This is the most modern method of dog training and, with a little practice, it is extremely effective as well as fun. The clicker is a small tool, which is about 5 x 3cm (2 x 1in) x 1.5cm (¹/₂in) thick. In one side is a piece of spring steel which, when pressed, emits a sharp, penetrating clicking sound. The more sophisticated clickers incorporate a whistle, too. Clicker training is an excellent way of teaching your dog the sequence: command, click, reward.

Start training

First teach your dog that a click means a reward by conditioning him to the click connecting the action with the reward. To do this, find a small place for just the two of you. Get his attention, click once and immediately give him a treat. Do this a dozen times until he associates a click with getting a treat.

The next stage

Using this method, you can teach your dog to sit, lie down, come when he is called, and stay, etc. on command. The following exercise illustrates how it works in practice. For example, to teach your dog to go into the 'down' position, you do the following.

1 Start with your dog in front of you in the 'sit' position.
2 Hold a tasty treat between your thumb and forefinger and allow him to sniff it.
3 Slowly move the treat straight down towards his front paws.
4 As he follows the treat with his nose, he should slide into a 'down' position automatically. Click and treat the moment he does so.

Note: Don't worry if this takes a few attempts before he gets the hang of it. Just be patient and repeat as necessary.

Taking it further

Once your dog is reliably offering the behaviour every time, you can start to add the command 'Down'. As he learns the verbal cue, start to reduce the food lure until he can perform the behaviour on the verbal cue only, without a treat. This is a simple, effective and kind method of teaching a dog. For information on how to obtain a clicker, see page 126.

Children

Some people think that this breed is not suitable for families with children under six years of age. It goes without saying that no young child should ever be left unattended with any dog, and an active Jack Russell is no exception. Children of any age should be taught not to over-excite or irritate the dog. If they poke him in the eye, he knows only one way to retaliate or defend himself – biting. The best way to educate children is to train them with the dog, so they learn to respect each other. Many obedience

clubs have introduced the Good Citizen for children and adults. Dogs benefit by being socialized with humans and other dogs. Children are motivated by winning medals with certificates. Perhaps more exciting are the clubs that teach Agility and Flyball. Both of these demand a lot of energy, and are enjoyed by children and adults as well as their Jack Russells.

Pest control

The Jack Russell requires no training to hunt – he is genetically programmed. However, an older, experienced dog may be used to accompany a young dog into a rat-infested building. It doesn't take long for the youngster to learn and become as efficient as his teacher. Before embarking on ratting, ensure your dog's vaccination against leptospirosis is up to date. This killer disease is spread in rats' urine. If you live in the UK, you should be aware

Jack Russells love playing with children, but they must learn to respect their dog.

that in January 2004 the Hunting Act came into force, which made it an offence to hunt any wild animal with dogs, although there are a few exceptions to this, which include pest control. The exemptions are as follows:
• Stalking and flushing out
• Using a dog below ground in the course of stalking and flushing out to protect birds that are being kept or preserved for shooting
• Hunting rats and rabbits permitted on land owned by the hunter or on land where the owner has granted permission in writing.

Note: The law in Scotland is slightly different; it allows an unlimited number of dogs for stalking and flushing.

Your responsibilities

Owners have to accept certain responsibilities, and for peace of mind here is a useful check list:

DO have your dog micro-chipped or tattooed
DO have an escape-proof garden
DO train children not to leave gates and doors open
DO walk your dog on a long retractable lead
DO have a pen or crate in the house to put him in for short periods when you go out
DO put your dog's toys in the pen, otherwise he may suffer separation anxiety and will find something else to do like chewing the furniture. As he gets older, he will stop
DO put him in a box or cage of the correct size when travelling.

DON'T leave food where your dog can reach it – it is too tempting
DON'T let him run free to chase cars, cyclists or joggers
DON'T take him out without a lead
DON'T leave him in the garden when the bin men or the postman call at your house
DON'T leave him in the garden when you are out – dog thieves may be watching
DON'T leave him alone for long periods
DON'T leave him in a car in hot weather – it can be very dangerous.

Curing problem behaviour

Even the best-trained Jack Russells can sometimes exhibit problem behaviours, but socializing your puppy (see page 42) and instilling good manners and desirable behaviour at an early age will help to prevent problems later on in adulthood. While your puppy is young, reward him when he behaves well and stop him doing the following:

• Jumping up at people
• Begging for food or stealing it
• Barking excessively
• Chewing and marking inside the house
• Growling at other dogs or people
• Chasing cyclists, joggers, etc.

Remember that some aspects of dog behaviour that we perceive as problems are totally natural for some breeds and we need to understand why they behave in this way and not to punish them for it. For example, it is natural for Terriers to dig and, unfortunately, you may never find a way of stopping your Jack Russell excavating your garden and digging up your favourite plants.

As a good owner, you should establish a good relationship with your dog and promote and reward desirable behaviour. Your dog will want to please you, and if you stop bad habits forming when he is still young, you can encourage good behaviour more easily and reward it.

House soiling

House training your puppy should prevent this problem (see page 36). However, some well-trained dogs can suddenly start soiling inside the house, often for no apparent reason. To resolve

Clean up

Always clean up any indoor mess thoroughly to remove any lingering smells. Don't use ammonia based cleaning products, but buy specially formulated ones for pets, which work more effectively.

this problem, you must find out why your dog is behaving in this way. There may be many reasons for this, including:

- Illness
- A change in diet
- Changes in his usual routine
- Boredom and being shut up alone for long periods
- Scent marking in male dogs.

If you think that your dog may not be well, consult your vet. Make sure that your dog has plenty of exercise and opportunities to toilet outside. Always take him out first thing in the morning and last thing at night, after eating, drinking and sleeping. If your male dog appears to be scent marking his territory indoors, then think about what may be triggering the behaviour. If it becomes excessive, ask your vet for advice.

Play biting

Don't be alarmed if your puppy is sometimes more inclined to nip you than to be affectionate when you want to give him a cuddle. Play biting is

You must discourage your dog from jumping up to greet you, other family members and visitors, however friendly he may be.

perfectly normal behaviour for puppies and not a sign of aggression, but it can be very painful, even though his teeth are still quite small. Until his adult teeth start coming through after four months, he will be teething and the pain will make him want to gnaw things – toys, furniture, your hands, etc. Also, puppies often play quite roughly with their litter mates and have to learn that they cannot treat you in the same way.

Terriers tend to bite more than other breeds of dog, so if your puppy play bites, cry out sharply and over-exaggerate the pain you feel. Encourage him to be gentle when playing games with toys and to give them up to you when he is asked (see page 74). If he continues to bite, then it is important that you stop the game immediately and remove the toy. In addition, you should provide your puppy with a variety of edible chews to cut his teeth on.

Escaping

Jack Russells are great escapologists and, no matter how happy they are are home, they will seize any opportunity to slip out of their garden and roam the local streets or countryside. You can help to prevent this by making sure your garden is escape-proof, repairing any gaps in the fences and raising their height, blocking up holes in hedges and placing wiring underneath gates. Also make sure that your dog has an up-to-date identity disc on his collar which is engraved with your telephone number just in case he still manages to escape.

Both bitches and dogs will sometimes escape to look for mating partners. Male dogs can smell a bitch on heat from up

However happy Jack Russells are in their own home and garden, many still yearn for the big wide spaces of the outside world.

to two miles away. However, some dogs will run away because they are bored at home and are seeking excitement. Jack Russells are active working dogs and they like to be busy, so make sure you put aside some time every day to play with your dog and perhaps teach him some simple tricks or go to Flyball or Agility classes. Your dog needs to be mentally and physically stimulated.

Jumping up

Jack Russells are naturally boisterous and some get very excited when visitors come to the house, jumping up enthusiastically

If your dog tends to get very excited to see you and jumps up when you come home, get down to his level to greet him.

toys or edible chews to keep him occupied in your absence. And before you leave, make sure that you play a game with him or take him out for a walk or run to tire him out. If you are going to be away from home for a few hours, it may be a good idea to arrange for a friend or neighbour he knows well to pop in and play with him or even to take him out for a walk or into the garden to relieve himself.

Aggression

Jack Russells are friendly and confident dogs if they have been socialized well as puppies. However, it is a sad fact that some dogs do display aggression occasionally towards other dogs or people, and this is never acceptable. Socialization is always the answer, and this should start at the earliest possible age. You need to introduce your dog to lots of other dogs, preferably on neutral territory away from your own home, which he will regard as his territory. Take him to training and obedience classes, and let him meet lots of people. Make sure that you always praise and reward his good behaviour with them.

to greet them. This can be annoying or even frightening for some people, so you must stop your dog doing this. One way of teaching your Terrier not to jump up is to crouch down and make a fuss of him when he greets you.

Alternatively, tell him firmly to 'Sit' (see page 39) and then, when he does so, make a fuss of him and give him a tasty treat to reward his good behaviour. He will soon learn to do this on command when visitors come to your home.

He will soon learn that the world is not such a frightening place as he thought and that contact with other dogs and people can be both enjoyable and rewarding.

If you continue to have problems, however, despite all your best efforts to resolve them, then talk to your vet. You may need to seek the professional advice and help of a trained pet behaviour counsellor (see page 126).

Destructive behaviour

Terriers are active dogs with a strong working instinct and they can get bored easily if they have nothing to do. This can trigger different types of problem behaviour, including chewing furniture and other items, or noisy barking.

To prevent this happening, whenever you go out, leave your dog some safe

Chapter 5

Dog showing

'Why don't you show him?' If you have a good-looking dog, you will be asked this question many times when you go to training classes, but beware – this simple question has changed the lives of thousands of people. Dog showing is peculiarly addictive and once the bug has really bitten, your life can be taken over.

You may find yourself reading about them, studying your own breed in detail, looking at videos, devouring the canine newspapers and attending seminars. If you have a competitive nature, you will want to win, and there's no stopping some owners once they get started. Many people's main aim is to show at Crufts for which they need to qualify by winning certain classes at Championship Shows. The next step may be to get onto club committees or to become judges. Climbing that ladder will lead some fortunate and talented enthusiasts to once-in-a-lifetime overseas judging appointments in exotic places.

Starting out

However, before anything exciting can happen you have to start with a dog who is good enough to compete. First of all, study the Standard carefully and evaluate your dog against it. Be honest with yourself and do not ignore your dog's faults and their seriousness – to do so is known as 'kennel blindness'. You may choose not to see the faults but a good judge will notice them, and a serious fault will prevent you winning. Discuss your dog with the instructors at your training club, but unless they are Terrier people they may not be able to help much.

Different types of show

Depending with which authority your dog is registered, you have the choice of two types of show in which to compete. Dealing with the Parson Russell Terrier first, you can show him in the more formal beauty shows licensed by the Kennel Club of which there are many all over Britain. Your dog will need to be Kennel Club registered and transferred to your name.

However, if you are registered with the Jack Russell Terrier Club of Great Britain (JRTC of GB) you will have agreed not to show at any Kennel Club

Opposite: Dog showing can be great fun, especially if your dog wins. However, win or lose, you always take the best dog home.

events. Later in this chapter, the showing of the working Jack Russell under the JRTC of GB rules will be discussed (see page 93). One thing is certain – owning a Jack Russell not registered with the Kennel Club does not make him inferior in any way; in fact, there are experienced Terrier people who believe theirs is the original breed and by far the best.

Watch the dogs in action

Bearing in mind the two Standards, you must aim to see as many as dogs as possible. Start off by going to one of the big Championship Shows licensed by the Kennel Club that have Parson Russell Terriers scheduled. You will find details of the shows in the weekly canine newspapers (see page 126) or on the internet. Just telephone the secretary for

a schedule. Conversely you can log onto the Championship society's website and download the schedule and entry form.

When you arrive at the show, find the breed ring and then watch the dogs in action, making notes of how they are handled, how they are walked and presented to the judge and, most importantly, how they look when they are groomed for exhibition. Take some photos to remind yourself which dogs win in the ring.

Try to make friends with some of the exhibitors, but make sure that you only approach them when they have finished with the judging. In the period that

At home, you can practise handling your dog in the show ring and standing him correctly for examination by the judge.

immediately precedes their class, many exhibitors are nervous and too busy preparing their dog to have time to talk to you, so wait until they have finished and then open the conversation by admiring their dog, which usually breaks the ice. An invitation to a glass of beer or a cup of tea also works wonders.

Importance of ringcraft

You can learn at a local training club the ringcraft that is necessary for success in the show ring. For instance, you need to know how fast to walk your dog, how to handle him on the table and how to present him and yourself to the judge. Serious beginners can reinforce this training at home by setting up a mock show ring in their garden and practising a couple of times a day with their dog. Ask some people you know to play the part of the judge, so that you can get your dog accustomed to being handled by various strangers.

Children enjoy this game but do make sure that the dog is always handled gently – any harshness at this juncture will be rewarded by a dog refusing to show. A Jack Russell has a long memory and is very pig headed once he is upset. At the club sessions, you will learn the etiquette of dog showing, the unwritten rules and the need for sportsmanship as well as the jargon that is used.

Schedules and entry forms

You might think there is a maze of regulations through which to thread your way, and to a certain extent this is true, but help is at hand in the shape of the experienced people at your training club. The show schedule will contain a definition of the classes together with which ones are available and an entry form. However, three things are of ultimate importance:

1 The entry form must be accurately completed or you may find either that you are not entered or, if you are lucky enough to win anything, you may be disqualified.

2 Remember to enclose the entry fees.

3 Post the completed form back before the closing date.

Note: Some shows now accept entries and payment on line. Be aware also that if you fail to turn up at the show, there is no refund of entry fees.

CCs

Not all shows, despite the appellation 'General Championship Shows', give awards that contribute to the championship status of any dog. Shows which schedule certain breed classes with Challenge Certificates on offer can describe themselves as Championship Shows. Which breeds get them is up to the show management but within the limits set by the Kennel Club. There are four exceptions: Crufts, Scottish Kennel Club, Welsh Kennel Club and Birmingham National. By Kennel Club regulation, these clubs must offer CCs to every breed that is entitled to receive them.

In-house matches

Having had some basic training at the ringcraft class, you will probably want to compete in your club's monthly matches. These are confined to club members, but sometimes they will compete against another training club.

In these elimination competitions, the dogs are matched against each other in pairs, the winner going on to the next round, and the process continues until one winner emerges at the end.

Companion Shows

After experiencing an in-house match, it would be wise to try out your new-found skills at the nearest and cheapest show where you will go against dogs that you have never seen under a judge who has never seen your dog. Remember that at the same time as honing your skills, you need to fine-tune those of your dog, introducing him to new sights and sounds.

Try a Companion Show where there is no advanced entry, and the entries are made on the day at the side of the ring. There will be four or five pedigree classes as well as a number of novelty classes, including ones for children. Champions and those dogs that have awards which contribute to their championship are not allowed to compete.

If the show is held at an agricultural show, there will be crowds of people, unusual noises from animals and farm machinery, and the ring will probably be harsh grass and not the smooth surface your dog is used to – all valuable experience. Winners of classes usually get a small amount of prize money.

Companion Shows are often held in conjunction with local agricultural shows, fêtes and the like, although sometimes they are staged in their own right. They are held under the auspices of the Kennel Club and should be licensed by them, and although any dog, registered or not, is entitled to enter, profits go to specified charities.

Primary Shows

These are for dogs beginning their show career who have never won a first prize except in the various puppy classes. On weekdays these shows cannot start before 5pm, but at weekends and bank holidays they can start at 2pm. There are no formalities for entries, which are taken at the show. At this point, you may be wondering why a show is advertised as an 'all breed Open or Championship Show' and your breed does not appear in the schedule. As the Kennel Club recognizes nearly 200 breeds it would not be possible to schedule them all. This is overcome by scheduling 'any variety not separately classified' and/or 'any variety'. In either class you will be competing with dogs of other breeds, but no Challenge Certificates will be on offer for these particular classes.

Limit Shows

Going up the scale there is the Limit Show, which is limited to members of the staging club, and you can join with your entry. There are not many of these shows but they are a useful step because you compete against dogs on your own level due to the fact that the winners of

Challenge Certificates, which go towards a dog's championship, and full champions are not allowed to compete.

Showing is addictive and it can become a very enjoyable part of your life together, even more so if your dog is a natural winner.

Open Shows

Next are the Open Shows, which are open to all recognized breeds, including champions although no CCs are on offer. Then there are breed Open Shows (no CCs) and breed Championship Shows (CCs), Group Open Shows (no CCs), Group Championship Shows (some breeds without CCs), Championship Shows and General Championship Shows (some breeds without CCs).

Breed Groups

A few words on the subject of Breed Groups: dogs have been split into groups to facilitate their administration. Most breeds fall naturally into groups that depict their function, i.e. the Terrier Group, Gundog Group, Toy Group, Hound Group, Pastoral and Working Groups. The Utility Group is composed of breeds that the canine authorities find difficult to fit into a given classification accurately.

Classes

There are many different classes available for shows to schedule, which are usually determined by the numerical strength of the breed. Definitions of classes appear in the schedules; with a few exceptions they are dominated by previous wins. Some exhibitors concentrate on winning their way out of the classes while others enter any class for which they qualify in the hope of winning, perhaps on the basis that the judge may favour their type regardless of previous wins.

There are four classes that are age related, and these are as follows:
1 Minor puppies from six to nine months old.
2 Any puppy from six to twelve months.
3 The junior class is for any dog up to 18 months of age, excluding champions and those who have won some certificates towards their championship.
4 The last class is for veterans – the usual age is for dogs over seven years of age. On the surface, these definitions can appear quite complicated and care should be taken to study them carefully and enter the right class, as any mistake can cause problems and may end up with a disqualification of a win.

In ordinary classes, Kennel Club show dogs are placed first, second, third, Reserve and Highly Commended. At Championship Shows, Challenge Certificates (CCs), which are known colloquially as 'tickets', are on offer to specified breeds. Three CC's given by three different judges will (subject to confirmation) get a dog its champion status. At least one must be awarded after the dog is one year of age. A reserve CC is on offer for both dogs and bitches, and if, by chance, the winner of the CC is disqualified, then the reserve winner will be upgraded. It is within the power of the judge to withhold awards if, in his opinion, the exhibits lack the required quality.

Once a year the allocation of Challenge Certificates to the breeds is published in the *Kennel Gazette*.

Preparing for a show

There are two main reasons for taking a dog to a dog show: one is to enjoy a social day out with people who have similar interests; another is to satisfy a competitive urge to win. It behoves you, therefore, to prepare both yourself and your dog as well as you can.

You will have trained your dog to perform in the ring but he needs to be groomed and trimmed on a par with his competitors. In a Kennel Club show, the presentation is more formal than in shows staged by the Jack Russell Club (JRTC of GB), and the dogs are usually trimmed to a greater degree. This is due to the fact that the priorities are slightly different and more perceived beauty comes into the equation. At the JRTC shows the priority is simply function. However, the dog should be clean and his coat should be tidy according to the current practice – there's no point in presenting your dog in a radical trim to judges who tend to be conservative.

As an exhibitor and judge, the author believes that presentation is important for you as well as your dog. Respect is due to the breed, the organizers of the show and the judge, so smart casual clothing is recommended for men while many women opt for trouser suits.

Be careful when choosing the colour of your clothes: it would not be sensible to show a white dog against some white clothes as he will probably be invisible.

As a judge looks at an exhibitor and their dog from an overall point of view subconsciously, they will prefer a more harmonious picture, so why not give it to them? It might just give you the edge on the other exhibitors and their dogs.

At the show

Some people go to a show armed with a brush and comb only, whereas others load up for any emergency. However, there is a middle way, and as you may be leaving early in the morning, it is wise to get everything ready the night before. Nothing is more irritating than arriving at a show having forgotten something important. Here is a useful check list of basic items to help you get ready:

Showing your dog can be great fun for both of you and can become a rewarding hobby. It is a great opportunity to make friends.

- Travelling crate
- Vetbed
- Grooming table/trolley
- Grooming tools
- Brush and comb
- Ring number clips
- Vacuum flask and cups
- Wallet or purse, credit cards, cash
- Dog food, water and dishes
- Documents, entry tickets and pen.

For a fast morning getaway, you should load the car the night before, except for the vacuum flask, your wallet and documents, etc. Fill the car with

Your car

If you are serious about dog shows you should have a reliable car and subscribe to a 'Get you home' service. Breaking down 100 miles from home on a cold night with two or three dogs in the car is no joke. A little tip: make sure the service you use takes dogs, as some won't.

fuel, and check the oil, water and tyre pressures. At the crack of dawn, make the coffee or tea, fill the flask, check your wallet, pick up your documents and then set off in good time.

Arriving at the show

Try and get to the show at least an hour before it starts. At KC Championship Shows buy a catalogue if you have not pre-paid for one, find out where you are supposed to be, then settle down and take your dog for a quick walk. Allow him to relieve himself in the designated place; if he makes a mistake, pick up the mess – you can be disciplined if you fail in this task. Give him some water brought from home, as local water might upset his stomach, and brush and comb him. Find out where your ring is and the time your classes are to be judged.

The ring steward will call the number of the class, the exhibitors will enter the ring and stand where they are told by the steward, who checks each number. Every judge has his own system, but described here is one of the most usual. The judge asks all the exhibitors to walk round the ring, following each other. He will ask one to put their dog on the table while the remainder stop and wait. The exhibitor presents his dog on the table to the judge, who will examine the dog's teeth, eyes, ears and head shape. He then goes over the animal's body and legs with his hands, checking the bone structure and the musculature.

He will ask the exhibitor to walk their dog in a pattern – this can vary but it is usually in the shape of a triangle. The dog is then taken back to his place, and every other dog is examined similarly. At the end the judge selects his first to fifth and then the next class is called. After all the dogs and bitches have been examined, the judge will select his best dog and bitch and finally which one will get the coveted Best of Breed award.

Grooming

The way in which you groom your dog will depend very much on his coat type and what sort of show he is entering.

Smooth coats

If your Jack Russell has a smooth-type coat, it will be harsh to the touch and the easiest of all the coats to maintain. A weekly brush will get rid of any dead hairs and let the new hair grow through, and you can shorten the moulting period if you brush it daily.

If you happen to be showing your dog, a good rub over with a slicker or hound glove – a mitten made of a fabric which polishes the coat by spreading the natural oils – will give it a sheen and thus show it to its best advantage.

Wire coats

The wire coat or, as it is often known, the rough coat can present problems. If left, it grows shaggy and can matt, as it does not moult. You can keep it tidy by combing with a close-toothed comb to get rid of some of the undercoat and by hand plucking the longer hairs. This is easily achieved by taking hold of some pelt between your finger and thumb (not so hard as to hurt the dog) in front of where you want to work, with the other hand using finger and thumb to pull out half a dozen hairs. Don't jerk – just pull firmly in the direction in which the hair grows and it will not hurt the dog. Work gently over the whole dog in this way.

Providing you start when your dog is young, he will not object. It is not difficult to do and the best way to learn is to get the breeder to show you or a good experienced exhibitor. If you do not want to do it yourself, you can visit a professional dog groomer once every three to four months. However, they will probably clip the dog, but that may alter the texture of the coat and make it softer. This does not matter very much for a pet dog but it may damage the prospects of a show dog.

Broken-haired coats

The broken-haired coat, which moults slightly, is a softer coat and it can grow quite long. This can be treated in the same way as a rough-coated dog. This type of coat is not mentioned in the Kennel Club Standard.

These Parson Russells are in show condition. Their coats do not need much attention before a big show – just a quick polish.

Grooming your dog

If you want to show your dog, you will need to keep his coat in good condition. Although the coat can be clippered and scissored to shape, this softens the texture, making it water absorbent, and any colour may be diluted. Hand stripping is essential for working and show dogs to maintain texture and colour. The difference between dogs prepared for JRTCGB shows and KC shows is the latter are more formal. It is not difficult to acquire the skills of stripping (sometimes alluded to as trimming) a rough or broken-haired coat – ask a friendly breeder for advice.

I When stripping the dog's body, only a few hairs are removed at one time. The other hand holds the skin just above the area being plucked.

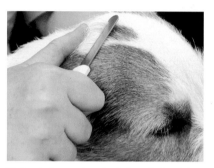

2 The hair on the dog's head should be kept short and merged seamlessly into the longer hair growing on the back of the neck.

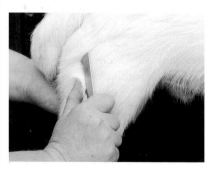

3 Carefully pluck the long hairs from behind the back legs, a few at a time, to show the dog's hind angulation. Hold the dog still while you do so.

4 With round-ended scissors, trim the hair around the feet to make them cat-like. Trim the hair underneath the feet between the toes.

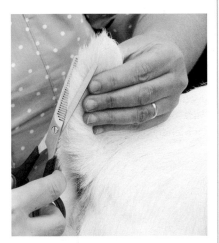

5 Use thinning shears under the tail and anus: it's too sensitive to pluck. Keep it short on the back of the tail, merge into the sides and trim the tip.

6 Daily and after every grooming session brush the dog's coat with a steel-toothed brush to remove the dead undercoat.

Working dogs

For a working dog, the coat is of great importance for he has to work in all weathers. There should be a good soft undercoat for its thermal qualities and a top coat for protection against heavy cover. It should easily reject water, so that in bitter cold weather it does not freeze in the coat with ice impeding the dog's movement and his ability to work.

Other shows

The JRTC of GB was set up in 1974 by eminent Terrier men to set the Standard and maintain the working characteristics of the real Jack Russell Terrier. They were perturbed that any small Terrier was being described as a Jack Russell and were determined to bring the breed up to what it should be historically. As the significant last sentence of the Standard states: 'A Jack Russell Terrier should not show any strong characteristics of another breed'. The founders feared that irresponsible breeding would dilute the innate working qualities of the breed. They also believed that should the breed be recognized by the Kennel Club and the Federation Canine International (FCI) or their affiliates, the emphasis of the breeders would change to meet the requirements of the show ring and few, if any, owners would risk their big show winners in a working environment. Thus, in the long run, Jack Russells would lose their intense genetic urge to hunt.

This belief is embodied in the Constitution of the JRTC of GB. Rules 2c,d,e and f, are explicit in their condemnation of anything they believe

Jack Russell Terriers will enjoy competing in JRTC events and activities with their owners.

to be to the detriment of a Jack Russell's ability and willingness to work. Rule 15 forbids any member to participate in a Jack Russell event or activity connected to a 'Conflicting Organization', and any Jack Russell registered with a Conflicting Organisation cannot be shown at any show under the JRTC of GB's rules. The club's definition of a Conflicting Organization is, 'Any Jack Russell Club that is registered with a KC or FCI related organization'. For administrative purposes, the JRTC has divided Great Britain into five regions, each of with its own secretary, staging two to four shows annually. The mother club stages its own annual National Show.

The shows staged by the regions under the JRTC of GB are much more 'laid back' than KC shows. They have a good ambience and the participants are friendly and helpful to the novice. Any dog can be entered, whether or not he is a member of the JRTC and the only proviso is that you are not a member of a conflicting organization. However, only members can compete in the various championship classes.

The classes are divided into two sizes:
- 25–31cm (10–12^1/$_2$ in)
- 31–37cm (12^1/$_2$–15in) in both dogs and bitches.

Note: Further divisions are between different coat types. There are also puppy classes as well as plenty of child handling classes.

Field trials

Because of the worry that the Jack Russell's natural impulse to hunt may become diluted, some countries have devised a system of field trials to train and test their ability and desire to go to earth without the inherent risks of the natural method. The Americans argued that all Terriers developed for specific purposes, and few actually do the work for which they were intended. They devised a competition to remind breeders what the real Terrier was all about. After all, 'What is a Terrier if he cannot hunt?'

The American Working Terrier Association was the first organization to build an acceptable artificial 'earth', consisting of a shallow trench with three 90-degree bends and three-sided wooden liners forming the tunnel. At one end, the tunnel is open for the Terrier to enter, while at the other there is an open space with a strong cage containing the quarry. The tunnel is covered with earth to look as natural as possible, and is scented with animal aroma. Live quarry (e.g. rats, rabbits, etc.) is used, although the Terrier is not allowed to get at it.

There are four tests – Novice Puppy, Novice Dog, Open Dog and Champion Dog. The trials get progressively more difficult as a dog wins his way out of the lower classes, and the tunnel gets longer and more complicated. In Australia, similar Earthdog trials are scheduled but not using live quarry.

The best dog

Finally, remember that no matter how well your dog does, even if he does not win or get placed, the joy of showing lies in competing and the fun of it all. At the end of the day, the best dog is always the dog you take home with you.

EPILOGUE: The tale of Toby

Many are the stories told by Terrier men after a day's hunting with their Jack Russells. Their bravery, tenacity and endurance in the hunting field are beyond doubt, but few could match the tale of Toby, a six-month-old pet Jack Russell who was out walking with his owners one cold winter's morning in 2005.

They were on the cliffs at Devils Point in Devon, England, when Toby was suddenly frightened by gunfire from a nearby Royal Marine range and fell over the cliff edge into the sea 23m (70ft) below. His horrified owners thought he had been killed on the rocks but, fortunately, council workers had seen him go over and called the Ministry of Defence police who sent a launch to search for him.

He was eventually found, cold and wet, on a rock near Torpoint in Cornwall, one mile away. He had swum over one of the busiest stretches of freezing water round the British Isles, through passing warships, submarines, tankers, ferries and freighters. He was returned to his owners wrapped in a blanket none the worse for his adventure, wagging his tail – typical of the breed and a lesson to us all.

PART TWO

HEALTHCARE

As a good owner, it is your responsibility to keep your Jack Russell fit and healthy. If you follow the basic guidelines in this book and socialize him, feed him a nutritious diet, exercise him adequately, groom him and play with him, you can prevent many health problems. However, it is important that you learn to recognize the warning signs of common problems and diseases so that you can treat them yourself or seek professional help from your vet before they get worse. Prevention is always preferable to cure, and a healthy, contented dog will be your trusted companion for many years to come.

Signs of good health

WARNING SIGNS
Here are some of the signs of poor health that you should look out for. If you think your dog is unwell, contact your vet.

- Loss of appetite
- Asking for food but not eating
- Eating more without weight gain
- Sudden weight loss
- Increased or excessive thirst
- Reluctance to exercise
- Limping and holding up a paw
- Decreased agility
- Pain on movement
- Discharge from eyes and nose
- Persistent cough
- Bad breath
- Yellowish-brown, cracked or missing teeth
- Bleeding, swollen or sore gums
- Persistent scratching
- Obsessive licking
- Skin inflammation
- Skin abscesses
- Dull coat
- Bloated abdomen
- Dragging the hindquarters
- Diarrhoea
- Vomiting
- Constipation.

Anal region This should be clean without any faeces clinging to the fur. The dog should not lick this area excessively or drag his rear along the ground.

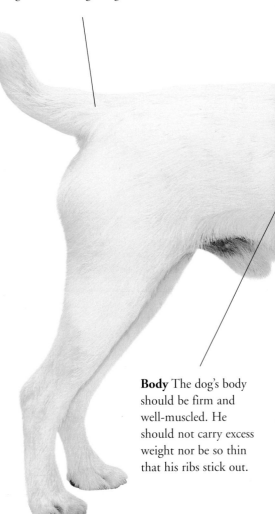

Body The dog's body should be firm and well-muscled. He should not carry excess weight nor be so thin that his ribs stick out.

Eyes The eyes should be bright, alert and with no signs of discharge, swelling or tear stains. A tiny amount of 'sleep' in the inner corners is quite normal.

Nose The nose of a healthy dog should be cold and damp without discharge. Occasionally there may be a little clear fluid.

Ears They should be responsive to any sound. The insides should be pale pink with no visible wax or unpleasant smell. Your dog should not shake his head or scratch his ears too often.

Teeth Healthy teeth are white and smooth, not yellow, which is a sign of plaque and tartar formation. The dog's breath should not smell unpleasant and there should be no loose or missing teeth or inflamed or bleeding gums.

Coat The coat should be in good condition and should smell pleasantly 'doggy'. It should be glossy and pleasant to touch. When you part the hairs, there should be no signs of fleas' droppings, sore or bare patches.

Claws The claws should end level with the pad and not be too long. Look out for broken claws, damage to dew claws (if they have not been removed) and hay seeds embedded in the pads.

Hereditary diseases

As in humans, dogs can inherit a wide range of diseases, and these may occur in pedigree and cross-bred animals. They are caused by genetic faults or aberrations in the breeding line. Although Jack Russell Terriers are basically strong and healthy characters, there has been an increase in the incidence of certain hereditary problems in some breeding lines. They include diseases of the heart, skeleton, nervous system, eyes and blood. None are very common but they all require immediate veterinary attention whenever the owner observes some abnormality in their pet.

Genetic faults

The genetic background to many hereditary ailments can be extremely complicated and is of concern to all breeders, veterinarians and geneticists. Screening tests are now available for tendencies to some hereditary diseases, and potential dog owners should consult their vet about possible inherited health problems within the breed and ask the breeder about the lineage and history of the dams and sires before purchasing a puppy. Although some hereditary diseases are treatable, the underlying genetic faults cannot be eliminated.

Hip joint problems

These are among the most common inherited diseases and can affect many breeds, including the two different types of Jack Russell (Parson Russell and the shorter-legged hunting type).

Legg-Calve-Perthes Disease

Commonly found in Jack Russells, this is a crumbling degeneration of the head of the femur (thigh bone) when its blood supply fails for reasons that are not yet understood. The symptoms, which begin after a puppy reaches six months of age, are progressive hindleg lameness and pain when the hip joint is touched. Treatment is by surgery to remove the diseased femoral head. After surgery the dog gradually returns to walking and running much as before, even though there is no bony joint in the hip. The muscles in the area form a synsarcosis, a substitute flexible attachment.

Hip dysplasia

In a normal, healthy dog, the hip is a 'ball and socket' joint, allowing a wide range of movement. The rounded end at the top of the femur fits tightly into the cup-shaped socket in the pelvis. In hip dysplasia, a shallow socket develops with a distorted femur head and slack joint ligaments. There can be excessive movement between the femur and pelvis, leading to a malfunctioning joint which will gradually become arthritic.

Early symptoms

If a puppy develops severe hip dysplasia, he may have some difficulty walking. Getting up from a sitting position may be painful and he will cry out. When he runs, he may use both hindlegs together in a 'bunny hop' or look as though he is swaying. These symptoms may be identifiable from five months onwards. Mildly affected puppies may show no signs at all of hip dysplasia at this age, but they will begin to develop arthritis at about eight years of age.

Hip dysplasia scheme

The British Veterinary Association and the Kennel Club run a joint scheme (the BVA/KC hip dysplasia scheme) based on hip scoring. The vet submits the X-ray, bearing the KC registration number of the dog, to the scheme. Each hip is then scored from 0 to 54, making a total of 108 maximum between the two hips. The lower the score the better, and 0:0 is the best score possible.

You should not breed from a dog or bitch with a higher hip score than the average for the breed or hip dysplasia will never be reduced or eliminated from that breed. When buying a puppy, always check that both the parents have been X-rayed, scored, and have achieved a low score. Although this does not guarantee that the puppy will not develop hip dysplasia at a later date, it does reduce the chances.

Treatment If mild hip dysplasia is treated in a growing puppy with anabolic steroids, limited exercise and diet, he will often grow into a healthy adult dog. However, you may have to restrict his exercise later on, too. In severe cases, surgery is available.

Luxation of the patella

This condition (dislocated kneecap) is a not infrequent disorder of both types of Jack Russell, which is also of genetic origin. The symptoms can be similar to those of Legg-Calve-Perthes Disease (see opposite). Again, treatment of persistent cases is surgical.

Hereditary ataxia

This serious genetic condition of the nervous system, with degeneration of areas of the cerebellum in the brain, causes a Jack Russell to display bouts of 'wobbliness', abnormal movements due to excessive tightening and spasm of leg muscles, a staggering gait and, sometimes, seizures. Eventually the dog cannot stand or even eat. The condition, which is recorded from time to time in both types of Jack Russell, can begin as early as two months of age. There is no effective treatment nor means of detecting carriers of the disease as yet.

Hydrocephalus

Another brain abnormality that sometimes occurs in both types of Jack Russell is hydrocephalus, which is a build-up of pressure within the organ, causing it to degenerate. The symptoms include disorientation and a tendency to bump into things when the dog is moving about. Normally, hydrocephalic dogs do not live very long. Unfortunately, there is no effective treatment for this condition.

Circulatory problems

Disease of the heart muscle of a congenital nature sometimes occurs. The symptoms include weakness or quickly becoming tired when exercising, wheezing and sudden collapse. Diagnosis requires prompt veterinary attention, and although treatment is often very effective it may have to be continued indefinitely. Similar symptoms in young dogs can be caused by a patent ductus arteriosus – the failure of a foetal blood vessel linking the aorta and pulmonary artery to close at birth. Here, surgery can be quite successful.

Von Willebrand's Disease

An occasional inherited bleeding disorder of both types of Jack Russell is Von Willebrand's Disease. Due to an insufficiency of a particular protein needed by the blood platelets circulating in the dog's vascular system, the ability of the blood to clot is diminished. Affected dogs bleed easily and for much longer than normal after a small wound.

They may suffer recurrent nose bleeds, bleeding gums and bloody urine. A veterinarian can test a dog for this disease, and such testing is invaluable where breeding is contemplated. The condition can be controlled effectively by medication.

Cryptorchidism

This is an inherited condition where one or both testicles have not descended by the time the puppy is six months old, and it is relatively common in Jack Russells and Parson Russells. An undescended testicle is non-functional but a potential source of problems later in life, particularly of becoming cancerous. Removal of both testicles by surgical castration is recommended.

Preventing disease

Check your dog

Do this regularly to spot potential problems – a grooming session is a good opportunity to examine your dog.
1 Look inside his mouth, checking that his teeth are clean and white and that his breath does not smell unpleasant. Clean the teeth with special toothpaste at least once a week.
2 Next check his eyes, nose and ears for signs of any discharge, odour or inflammation. Keep them clean by wiping them gently with some damp cotton wool.
3 Examine the dog's coat, looking for bald patches, excessive hair loss, tell-tale signs of fleas (black sooty specks in the

fur) and soiling around the anus and rear end. The coat should always look healthy and glossy, and the dog should not scratch excessively.
4 Pick up each of his paws and check the pads and claws, which should not be broken nor too long. If your dog appears to be limping, look for cuts or any swellings on the pads. Some dogs are susceptible to grass and hay seeds becoming embedded in their pads.

Note: If you find anything unusual or suspect there may be a health problem, then make an appointment to take your dog to the vet. Even if it is only a minor worry, this will set your mind at rest.

You can treat the problem before it gets more serious and learn how to prevent it recurring in the future.

Vaccinations

The most important thing you can do to protect your dog's health is to make sure that he is vaccinated against the major infectious canine diseases. These are distemper, infectious canine hepatitis, 'kennel cough', parvovirus and the two forms of leptospirosis. Vaccination against all these serious ailments can be given by your vet in one shot when a puppy is at least six weeks of age. A second dose is administered three to six weeks later. An annual booster dose is recommended thereafter to top up your dog's immunity, although some veterinary authorities believe this is not necessary. However, like most vets, I personally am in favour of it.

In some countries vaccination of dogs against rabies is obligatory. Puppies can be vaccinated as early as four weeks of age. Yearly booster shots are essential.

Pet Passports

If you are considering taking your dog on holiday to one of the European Union countries or to certain other designated rabies-free countries, you must obtain a Pet Passport. The same applies to dogs travelling abroad to dog shows and competitive events. Your vet and the local DEFRA office will give you information on how to go about this. The dog will have to be micro-chipped, vaccinated against rabies and blood tested 30 days after vaccination before you leave for your trip, and then treated against ticks and other parasites 24 to 48 hours before your return with a veterinary certificate to prove it. You must have a DEFRA PETS re-entry certificate certifying that the blood test gave a positive result for immunity against rabies after the vaccination, and you will have to sign a declaration that the dog did not leave the qualifying countries while you were away.

Neutering your dog

Unless you are definitely contemplating breeding from your dog, it is best, for the dog and for you, to have a bitch spayed or a dog castrated after they reach six months of age. Castration reduces aggressiveness and the likelihood of a male dog going a-roaming. Spaying, apart from avoiding the arrival of unwanted puppies, reduces the chances of breast tumours in later life and, obviously, the onset of common uterine disease, such as pyometra. Neither castration nor spaying change the character of dogs nor necessarily make them put on weight. Talk to your vet about what is involved.

Diet is important

Feeding a well-balanced, nutritious diet will help to keep your dog healthy. It is important not to over-feed him or he may gain too much weight and this can lead to many health problems that are associated with obesity as well as a reduced life expectancy. If you are unsure as to which foods, how much and how often to feed your dog, ask your vet. Similarly, if your dog loses his appetite or sheds weight suddenly, ask your vet's advice – the dog may well need worming (see page 105) or the symptoms may be a sign of a more serious underlying problem.

Carrying excess weight can put extra strain on a dog's joints and increase the chances of arthritis, heart disease or diabetes developing. Keep your pet slim and trim but, if he begins to pile on the pounds, follow my advice on page 116.

Keep your dog fit

All dogs need regular exercise every day to keep them fit and maintain optimum health. The Jack Russell, an exuberant, active, working breed, should walk and run many miles a day. He will lose his fine shape if he is not given plenty of vigorous exercise.

Stimulate your dog

Playing games with your dog and teaching him tricks will provide both mental and physical stimulation. Lively dogs like Jack Russells need to be busy and active, or they soon become bored and this can lead to behaviour problems as well as to poor health.

Parasites

Dogs can play host to two sorts of unwelcome parasite – external and internal ones. By worming your dog regularly and treating him with flea treatments, especially in the spring and summer, you can prevent infestations occurring and keep him healthy.

External parasites

These parasites live on the surface of the dog's body, and include lice, fleas, ticks, mites and ringworm (see page 117). Keep a look out for them and treat an infected dog as quickly as possible.

Fleas

Dogs are usually infested by their own, and the cat's, species of flea but they can sometimes carry rabbit, human or hedgehog fleas. The infestations are more likely to be worse in warm weather in the summer, but fleas thrive all the year round, particularly if your home has central heating. Sometimes it is extremely difficult to find any fleas on a dog, but just a single flea can cause an allergic reaction when piercing a dog's skin and injecting its saliva. Such a reaction can result in widespread irritation, skin sores and rashes. Flea eggs do not stick to the dog's hair like those of lice (see opposite), but, being dry, they drop off onto carpets and furniture.

COMMON SYMPTOMS
- **An affected dog will keep scratching**
- **Tiny reddish scabs or papules appear on the skin, particularly on the dog's back**
- **Flea droppings look like coal dust in the dog's coat.**

What you can do Use insecticidal sprays, shampoos or powders, which are obtainable from the vet, chemist or a pet shop, at regular intervals throughout the summer. Treat the floors, furniture and your pet's favourite sleeping places, basket and bedding with a specially formulated aerosol product every seven months. This procedure effectively stops the re-infestation of dogs by larvae emerging from eggs in the environment.

Lice

There are two kinds: biting lice which feed on skin scales; and sucking lice which draw tissue fluids from the skin. The latter cause more irritation to the dog than the former. Lice are greyish-white and about 2mm ($^1/8$in) in length. Their eggs (nits) are white and cemented to the dog's hairs. The dog louse does not fancy humans or cats and will not infest them.

COMMON SYMPTOMS
- **The dog will scratch himself**
- **Lice and nits will be visible to the naked eye when the dog's coat is carefully searched.**

What you can do Sprays, powders or baths are available from the vet or pet shop. Apply on at least three occasions at five- to seven-day intervals to kill adults and the larvae that hatch from the nits.

Ticks

More often seen on country dogs than town dogs, ticks suck blood, their abdomen swelling up as they do so. The commonest tick of dogs is the sheep tick. It clings to the dog's hair, generally on the legs, head or under-belly, and pierces the skin with its mouth parts. In doing so it can transmit an organism called Borrelia, a cause of Lyme Disease. Characterized by lameness and heart disease, it always requires veterinary

diagnosis by means of blood tests, and then treatment using specific antibiotics and anti-inflammatory drugs.

What you can do You can remove a tick by dabbing it with some alcohol, such as gin or methylated spirits. Wait a few minutes for its head to relax, and then, grasping it near to the mouthparts with some fine tweezers – you can buy special ones for this – dislodge the tick with a little jerk. Do not ever attempt to pull it off without applying the alcohol first as the mouthparts left in the skin may cause an abscess to form.

An alternative method is to spray the tick with some flea spray and then to remove it the following day. The regular application of a flea spray or fitting your dog with an insecticidal collar during the summer months is highly recommended in order to control tick infestation.

Internal parasites

These parasites live inside the dog's body. Several kinds of worm can infest dogs and, in very rare cases, these parasites can spread to human beings.

Roundworms

These live, when adult, in the dog's intestines but their immature forms migrate through their host's body, damaging such organs as the liver and lungs, particularly those of puppies.

Hookworms and whipworms

These blood-sucking parasites can cause severe anaemia. Your veterinary surgeon will be able to confirm if your dog is affected.

Tapeworms and roundworms

The commonest dog tapeworm, *Dipylidium*, is spread by fleas, in which its larvae develop. You can see the segments of this tapeworm looking like wriggling white grains of rice in droppings or stuck to the hair around the dog's bottom. Roundworms cause the most trouble for dogs, particularly puppies.

> **COMMON SYMPTOMS**
> • **Symptoms of roundworms include bowel upsets, emaciation, fits, chest and liver malfunction**
> • **Tapeworms may cause dogs to drag their rear ends ('scoot') along the floor.**

What you can do To treat roundworms, you should give your dog a 'worming' medication which will be available from your vet. Puppies usually should receive their first dose at three weeks of age. Repeat the worming every three weeks until they are 16 weeks old, repeating at six months and twice a year thereafter.

Give your dog anti-tapeworm medication once a year or when any worm segments are seen in his droppings or on the hair near and around the anus. Regular flea control will also help you to combat tapeworms. Some worm treatments are effective against all types of internal parasites, and you should consult your veterinary surgeon about which products are suitable and the correct dosage.

Dental care

Check your dog's teeth regularly and brush them once or twice a week to prevent any tartar building up. Gnawing on a variety of bones and chews will help to keep his teeth clean and healthy.

Tooth disease

It is relatively easy to spot the common symptoms of tooth disease and dental decay. They are listed in the box below.

> **COMMON SYMPTOMS**
> • **Your dog may salivate (slavering) at the mouth**
> • **He may paw at his mouth**
> • **Chewing motions may be exaggerated**
> • **He may chew tentatively as if he is dealing with a hot potato**
> • **His breath may smell unpleasant.**

What you can do Cleaning the teeth once or twice weekly with cotton wool or a soft toothbrush dipped in salt water (or specially formulated dog toothpaste) will stop tartar formation. 'Bones' and 'chews' made of processed hide (available from pet shops) and the occasional meal of coarse-cut, raw butcher's meat also helps.

Tartar

When tartar, a yellowy-brown, cement-like substance, accumulates, it does not produce holes in the teeth that need filling. Instead it damages the gum edge, lets in bacteria to infect the tooth sockets and thus loosens the teeth. Tartar will always cause some gum inflammation (gingivitis) and frequently bad breath. If your pet displays the symptoms described, open his mouth and look for a foreign body stuck between his teeth. This may be a sliver of wood or bone stuck between two adjacent molars at the back of the mouth or a bigger object jammed across the upper teeth against the hard palate. You can usually flick out foreign bodies with a teaspoon handle.

Gingivitis
Bright red edging to the gums where they meet the teeth, together with ready bleeding on even gentle pressure, are the principal signs of gingivitis (gum disease). Tap each tooth with your finger or a pencil. If there are any signs of looseness or tenderness, wash the dog's mouth with some warm water and salt, and give him an aspirin tablet – there is little else you can do without seeking professional help. Take the dog to the vet and ask his advice.

Broken teeth
Sometimes a dog will break a tooth, perhaps by fighting or chewing stones (a bad habit that some dogs get into). The large 'fang' teeth (canines) are most often the ones damaged. These injuries do not usually produce signs of toothache, root infection or death of the tooth. Treatments used in human dentistry, such as fillings, root treatments or crowning, may be necessary and are all possible.

Ulcers and tumours
Mouth ulcers, tumours (juvenile warts are common in young dogs) and tonsillitis will all need veterinary diagnosis and treatment where they are the cause of some of the symptoms mentioned above.

Canine dentistry
This is easily tackled by your vet. Using tranquillizers or short-acting general anaesthetics, tartar can be removed from a dog's teeth with scrapers or an ultra-sonic scaling machine. Antibacterial drugs may be prescribed if encroaching tartar has caused secondary gum infection. Bad teeth must be taken out to prevent root abscesses and socket infection from causing problems, such as septicaemia, sinusitis or even kidney disease, elsewhere in the dog's body.

Eye problems

Your dog's eyes are very precious and you must check regularly that they are normal and healthy.

Watering and discharge
If just one of the dog's eyes is involved and the only symptom is watering or a sticky discharge without any marked irritation, you can try washing the eye gently with boracic acid powder in warm

> **COMMON SYMPTOMS**
> • Sore, runny or 'mattery' eyes
> • Blue or white film over the eye
> • Partially or totally closed eye or eyes.

water once every few hours, followed by the introduction of a little Golden Eye ointment (which is obtainable from the chemist) onto the affected eyeball.

If any symptoms in or around the eyes last for more than a day, go to the vet. Particularly in young dogs, two mattery eyes may indicate distemper (see page 111).

Eye conditions

Persistent watering of one or both eyes can be due to a very slight infolding of the eyelid (entropion) or to blocked tear ducts. A blue or white film over one or both eyes is normally a sign of keratitis, which is an inflammation of the cornea. This is not a cataract but it does require immediate veterinary attention.

Cataract and luxation

Opacity of the lens (cataract) can be seen as a blue or white 'film' much deeper in the eye. The pupil looks greyish instead of the usual black. This usually occurs in elderly dogs but may be seen sometimes in young puppies (congenital cataract) and also at other ages (diabetic cataract). Jack Russells have a tendency to develop luxation (dislocation) of the lens in one or both eyes. Both cataract and luxated lens conditions can be treated by surgery.

Glaucoma

Increased pressure within the eye, glaucoma is a serious condition that can be hereditary in certain blood lines of Jack Russells or may follow some other form of eye disease. The first signs may be dilation of the pupil, cloudiness behind the cornea, enlargement of the blood vessels in the 'white' of the eye and pain, often manifested early on, by the dog rubbing his eye with a paw or against an object. The effect of prolonged high pressure within the eye is to produce

blindness. If spotted quickly, it can be controlled to a reasonable degree by medication, including special eye drops.

Progressive retinal atrophy (PRA)

This is occasionally found in both types of Jack Russell and is probably congenital. Dogs between three and five years of age begin to have difficulty seeing stationary objects and apparently see best in dim light. Both eyes are affected. The condition usually leads to complete blindness after a year or two, and there is no effective treatment.

Inflammations of the eye

These can be treated by the veterinarian in a variety of ways. Antibiotic injections, drops and ointments are available, plus various other drugs to reduce inflammation, as are surgical methods of tackling ulcerated eyes under local anaesthesia. Problems due to deformed eyelids, foreign bodies embedded in the eyeball and even some cataracts can all be treated surgically nowadays.

Entropion and distichiasis

In entropion, the edge of the eyelid folds inwards so the lashes rub against the eyeball itself. The eye becomes sore and weeps and may be kept closed. The condition can be corrected with surgery. An associated condition is distichiasis, where abnormal hairs growing on the inner surface of the eyelids cause irritation to the cornea that can lead to severe inflammation and ulceration. Again, treatment is by surgery or through electro-epilation, removing the hairs by destroying their roots.

Ear problems

A healthy dog's ears should be alert and responsive to sounds. The ear flaps of most breeds are usually pale pink and silky inside, and there should be no wax or nasty odour. A dog who keeps scratching his ears and shaking his head may have an ear infection.

> ## COMMON SYMPTOMS
> • Shaking the head and scratching the ear
> • It is painful when the ear is touched
> • There may be a bad smell and discharge
> • The dog tilts his head to one side
> • There is ballooning of the ear flap.

Preventing problems
Clean your dog's ears once a week. For dogs with hair growing in the ear canal, pluck out the hair between finger and thumb. Don't cut it. Using 'baby buds' or twists of cotton wool moistened in warm olive oil, clean the ear with a twisting action to remove excess brown ear wax. See the vet early with any ear trouble. Chronic ear complaints can be very difficult to eradicate.

Treating minor problems
If symptoms suddenly appear and the dog is in distress, an effective emergency treatment is to pour a little warmed (not hot) liquid paraffin carefully into the affected ear. Acute inflammation will be greatly soothed by the oil. Don't stuff proprietary liquids into a dog's ear; you do not know what you may be treating.

Most of all, avoid those so-called canker powders, as the powder bases of these products can cause additional irritation by forming annoying accumulations that act as foreign bodies.

Ear irritation
This may be due to various things that find their way into the ear canal. Grass awns may need professional removal. Small, barely visible white mange mites that live in dog's ears cause itching, and bacteria can set up secondary infections. Sweaty, dirty conditions provide an ideal opportunity for germs to multiply. The vet will decide whether mites, bacteria, fungi or other causes are the source of inflammation, and will use antiparasitic, antibiotic or antifungal drugs as drops or injections.

Middle-ear disease
Although tilting of the head may be due simply to severe irritation on one side, it can indicate that the middle ear, the deeper part beyond the eardrum, is involved. Middle-ear disease does not necessarily result from outer-ear infection but may arise from trouble in the Eustachian tube which links the middle ear to the throat. This will always require some rigorous veterinary attention with the use of antiflammatory drugs, antibiotics and, more rarely, deep drainage operations.

Ballooning of an ear flap
This may look dramatic and serious but in fact it is a relatively minor problem. It is

really a big blood blister, which is caused by the rupture of a blood vessel in the ear flap. It generally follows either some vigorous scratching where ear irritation exists or a bite from another dog. It can be treated surgically by the vet, who may drain it with a syringe or open it and then stitch the ear flap in a special way to prevent any further trouble.

Deafness

There is a breed predisposition to deafness in both types of Jack Russell with their predominantly white coat colouring. The origin is genetic with the deafness gene being linked to the gene for the white colour of the body hair, as is the case in other white animals, such as cats, which are also often deaf.

Nose problems

Don't allow your dog's nostrils ever to get caked and clogged up. Bathe them thoroughly with warm water and anoint the nose pad with some soothing cold cream. If there are any 'common cold' symptoms, you must seek veterinary advice immediately.

COMMON SYMPTOMS
- **The dog's nostrils are running and mattery**
- **The dog appears to have the equivalent of a human common cold**
- **The nose tip is sore, cracked and dry**
- **Check the eyes as well as the nose – if they are both mattery, the dog may have distemper.**

Sore noses

Old dogs with cracked, dry nose pads will need regular attention from their owners to keep their nostrils free and to deal with bleeding from the cracks. If this is the case, you should bathe your dog's nose frequently, applying cod liver oil ointment twice or three times daily and working it in well. Your vet may prescribe multivitamins or corticosteroid preparations for the condition.

Rhinitis and sinusitis

Symptoms such as sneezing, a mattery discharge from the nostrils, head shaking and, perhaps, nose bleed may indicate rhinitis (the inflammation of the nasal passages) or sinusitis (inflammation within one or more of the sinus chambers in the skull). Bacterial, viral or fungal germs, foreign bodies, growths, tooth abscesses or eye disease can be the cause of these conditions.

Like humans, dogs possess air-filled spaces in the bones of their skulls (sinuses) which can become diseased. Infections or tumours can occur in these cavities. Sometimes an infection can spread into them from a bad tooth root nearby. The signs of sinusitis include sneezing, persistent nasal discharge and head shaking. If you notice any of these symptoms, you should take your dog to the vet without delay. The treatment can involve anti-bacterial or anti-fungal drugs, surgical drainage or dental work as appropriate.

Respiratory problems

Dogs can suffer from bronchitis, pleurisy, pneumonia, heart disease and other chest conditions. Coughing and sneezing, the signs of a 'head cold', possibly together with mattery eyes, diarrhoea and listlessness, may indicate distemper – a serious virus disease.

COMMON SYMPTOMS
- **The dog may cough**
- **There may be some wheezing and sneezing**
- **The dog's breathing may be laboured.**

Distemper

Although this is more common in younger animals, it can occur at any age and shows a variety of symptom combinations. Dogs catching distemper can recover although the outlook is serious if there are symptoms such as fits, uncontrollable limb twitching or paralysis, which suggest that the disease has affected the nervous system. These may not appear until many weeks after the virus first invades the body.

What you can do Your dog should be vaccinated against distemper and other important canine viral and leptospiral diseases at the first opportunity – when he is a puppy and has reached six weeks of age – and make sure that you keep the annual booster dose going. At the first signs of any generalized illness, perhaps resembling 'flu' or a 'cold', contact the vet. Keep the dog warm, give him plenty of liquids and provide easily digestible nourishing food.

Your vet can confirm whether the dog has distemper. Because it is caused by a virus, the disease is very difficult to treat. Antibiotics and other drugs are used to suppress any dangerous secondary bacterial infections. Vitamin injections help to strengthen the body's defences. The debilitating effects of coughing, diarrhoea and vomiting are countered by drugs which reduce these symptoms.

Coughs

Where troublesome coughs occur in the older dog, give a half to two codeine tablets three times a day, depending on the animal's size, but see the vet.

Heart disease

This is common in elderly dogs and often responds well to treatment. Under veterinary supervision, drugs can give a new lease of life to dogs with 'dicky' hearts. It is useful in cases of heart trouble and in all older dogs to give vitamin E in the synthetic form (50–200mgm per day depending on the dog's size) or as wheat germ oil capsules (two to six per day).

Bronchitis

Inflammation of the tubes that conduct air through the lungs can be caused by a variety of bacteria and viruses, parasitic lungworms, allergy, inhalation of dust, smoke, foreign bodies or excessive barking. Specific therapy is applied by the vet and sometimes, in the case of foreign bodies, surgery or the use of a fibre-optic bronchoscope is necessary.

Pneumonia

There are many causes of pneumonia in dogs, the commonest being infections by micro-organisms such as viruses or bacteria. Migrating parasitic worm larvae and inhalation of foreign bodies are less frequent. The signs are faster and/or more laboured breathing, a cough, raised temperature and, often, nasal discharge. It can be treated with antibiotics,

corticosteroids, 'cough' medicines and medication to relieve the symptoms. Pneumonia always demands immediate professional attention.

Kennel cough

This is caused by a bacterium (*Bordetella*) or viruses (Canine parainfluenza virus, Canine herpes virus or Canine adenovirus) or a mixture of these. The signs are a dry cough, often with sneezing, and a moderate eye and nostril discharge. Dogs can be protected by special vaccines administered either by injection or, in some cases, as nasal drops.

Tummy problems

There are numerous causes for tummy troubles in a dog but if you are worried or the symptoms persist for longer than twelve hours, you should consult your veterinary surgeon. If your dog has a minor tummy upset, you could try feeding him some rice or pasta cooked with chicken, or some other bland meal.

COMMON SYMPTOMS
- An affected dog may experience vomiting, diarrhoea, constipation
- Blood in his droppings
- Loss of appetite and refusing food
- Flatulence may be present
- The dog may eat or drink more than normal
- He may drink less than normal.

Vomiting

Vomiting may be simple and transient due to either a mild infection (gastritis)

of the stomach or to food poisoning. If severe, persistent or accompanied by other major signs, it can indicate serious conditions, such as distemper, infectious canine hepatitis, an intestinal obstruction, leptospirosis or a heavy worm infestation. In this case, seek veterinary attention urgently. The usual treatment for vomiting is to replace lost liquids (see diarrhoea opposite) and give the dog one to three teaspoons of Milk of Magnesia, depending on his size, once every three hours.

Necrosis of the mandibular salivary glands

A curious and, fortunately, rather rare condition which has been reported in Jack Russells is necrosis of the mandibular salivary glands. Of so far unknown cause, the symptoms are dramatic enlargement of the glands under the lower jaw, together with continual retching and vomiting. Treatment is by symptomatic medication and, crucially, surgical removal of the glands.

Diarrhoea

This may be nothing more than the result of a surfeit of liver or a mild bowel infection. However, diarrhoea can be more serious and profuse where important bacteria are present, in certain types of poisoning and in some allergies. Again, you should take your dog to the vet as soon as possible.

For mild cases of diarrhoea, cut out solid food, milk and fatty things. Give your dog fluids – best of all are glucose and water or some weak bouillon cube broth – little and often. Ice cubes can also be supplied for licking. Keep the animal warm and indoors.

Constipation

If your dog is constipated and is not passing any stools, it may be due to age, a faulty diet including too much chomped-up bone, or to an obstruction. Don't use castor oil on constipated dogs. Give them liquid paraffin (a half to two tablespoons). Where an animal is otherwise well but you know he is bunged up with something like bone which, after being crunched up, will set like cement in the bowels, you could get a suitable enema from the chemist.

Flatulence

'Windy' dogs may be the product of a faulty or changed diet. Often flatulence is associated with food that is too low in fibre although, paradoxically, too much

fibre can have a similar effect. Generally, adjusting the dog's diet to one of high digestibility and low residue will do the trick. Adding bran to the dog's food will alleviate many cases.

Blood in the stools

This condition can arise from a variety of minor and major causes. It may be from nothing more than a splinter of bone scraping the rectal lining, or the cause may be more serious, such as the dangerous leptospiral infection. Your vet will be able to identify the cause and advise on suitable treatment.

Malabsorption

Some dogs with chronic diarrhoea, which is often rather fatty looking, associated with a strong appetite but loss of weight, are not able to digest or absorb their food normally. The causes include enzyme deficiency (liver or pancreas faults) or disease of the bowel walls. The vet will employ a variety of tests to establish the cause and prescribe the appropriate therapy. Dogs deficient in pancreatic enzymes can be given pancreatic extract supplements with their food.

Polydipsia and polyphagia

Both of these conditions – polydipsia (drinking more than normal) and polyphagia (eating more than normal) – can be associated with diabetes, disease of the adrenal glands, kidney disease and other conditions. Careful examination by the vet, together with laboratory tests on blood and/or urine samples, is necessary to pinpoint the cause and thus lead to the correct treatment.

Salmonella infection

Salmonella is a type of bacterium that occurs in a wide variety of strains (serotypes) which may cause disease in, or be carried symptomlessly by, almost any species of animal. Sometimes salmonella can be found in the droppings of apparently normal healthy dogs. Dogs can contract salmonellosis by eating infected food, especially meat and eggs, or by coming into contact with rodents or their droppings, other infected dogs or, more rarely, reptiles or birds. The most common symptoms include diarrhoea (sometimes bloody), vomiting, stomach pain and even collapse, sometimes ending in death. Diagnosis is confirmed by the vet sending away some samples for bacteriological culture and identification. Treatment is by means of specific antibiotics and fluid replacement. However, it is worth remembering that salmonella infection in animals may be transmissible to humans.

Parvovirus infection

This virus disease is spread via faeces. The incubation period is five to ten days and symptoms vary from sudden death in young pups, through severe vomiting, foul-smelling diarrhoea (often bloody), reduced appetite and depression to bouts of diarrhoea. Treatment includes replacing lost fluid, anti-vomiting and anti-diarrhoea drugs and antibiotics. Puppies can be vaccinated against parvovirus.

Acute abdomen

The sudden onset of severe pain, vomiting with or without diarrhoea and the collapse of the dog into shock is an emergency that necessitates immediate veterinary attention. The cause may be a powerful, rapidly-developing infection, obstruction of the intestine by a foreign body or a twist of the bowel itself, torsion (twisting) of the stomach, acute kidney, liver or uterine disease or poisoning. Successful treatment depends on quick diagnosis.

Urinary problems

Male dogs will urinate many times a day, in the course of a walk or a run in the garden. Bitches generally urinate less often. The usual signs of urinary disease are increased thirst and urination.

COMMON SYMPTOMS
• **Difficulty in passing urine**
• **Urination is frequent**
• **Blood is present in the dog's urine**
• **The dog may be more thirsty than usual.**

Types of urinary disease

If something is wrong with your dog's waterworks, see the vet. Inflammation of the bladder (cystitis), stones in the bladder and kidney disease are quite common and will need immediate professional advice. Whatever you do, don't withhold drinking water.

Leptospirosis

This is the most common disease of a dog's kidneys. Humans can be infected by contact with dogs who suffer from this. Symptoms can be acute with loss of appetite, depression, back pain, vomiting, thirst, foul breath and mouth ulcers, or more chronic with loss of weight and frequent urination. It can be diagnosed by blood and urine tests and treated with antibiotics. Vaccination is also available.

Cystitis

This inflammation of the bladder generally responds well to effective treatment with antibiotics, such as ampicillin, perhaps together with medicines that alter the acidity of the urine and urinary sedatives.

Calculi

A diagnosis of stones (calculi) in the urinary system can be confirmed by your vet. In most cases, they are easily removed surgically under general anaesthetic.

Kidney disease

Kidney disease always needs careful management and supervision of diet. Chronic kidney disease patients can live to a ripe old age if the water, protein and mineral content of the diet are regulated, bacterial infection controlled, protein loss minimized and stress of any sort avoided. Prescription diets for chronic kidney cases are available from the veterinary surgeon and good pet shops.

Skeletal problems

The most common skeletal problems in dogs are arthritis and slipped disc. Arthritis is much more common in elderly dogs than in young ones, and it invariably follows hip dysplasia.

COMMON SYMPTOMS
- **The dog may be lame**
- **He may have difficulty getting up**
- **His gait may be stiff, slow or unusual**
- **There may be painful spots on bones or joints.**

Arthritis

This painful condition may arise from the congenital weakness of certain joints, their over-use/excessive wear, injuries, infections and nutritional faults. Treatment is similar to that in humans, and your vet may well prescribe corticosteroids, non-steroidal anti-inflammatory drugs and various analgesics. Massages, perhaps with anti-inflammatory gels or creams, homoeopathic remedies and acupuncture can also afford relief and improved mobility in some cases. If you are considering trying out alternative medical treatment, consult your vet first.

You should avoid taking your dog out in very cold or wet weather, and buy him a snug coat for outdoor use. Provide daily multivitamins and minerals and give elderly dogs, in particular, one to four capsules or teaspoons (depending on size) of halibut liver oil.

Painful joints

Arthritis can result in the thickening of the joint capsule, abnormal new bone forming round the joint edges, and wearing of the joint cartilage. The joint becomes enlarged and painful and its movement is restricted. It tends to affect the shoulders, hips, elbows and stifles.

Obesity and joints

Carrying excess weight can put extra strain on a dog's joints. Slim down an overweight dog by modifying his diet (reducing carbohydrates and fats), feeding special canned slimming rations, desisting from giving him sweet titbits, and increasing his exercise gradually. Your vet may run a special slimming programme: expert guidance will be provided and your dog's progress will be monitored by regular weighing.

Slipped disc

A dog's adjacent spinal vertebrae are separated by discs shaped rather like draughts pieces, which act as shock absorbers when functioning correctly. With the passing of time, as dogs grow older, the discs lose their elasticity and become more brittle, less compressible and degenerated. Then, a sudden

movement or trauma can cause a disc to 'burst' with the discharge of crunchy material that piles up against the spinal cord or a nerve root with the consequent rapid onset of symptoms. The disc itself does not actually 'slip' out of line with the spine. Jack Russells as a breed are not as prone to 'slipped discs' as others, such as Dachshunds and Basset Hounds, with their long backs and short legs.

Symptoms and treatment

The signs of a slipped disc include sudden onset of neck or back pain, paralysis or weakness of the limbs, loss of sensation, limb spasms and loss of control of the bladder. Accurate diagnosis is aided by X-rays. Treatment is by means of medication (analgesics, sedatives, anti-inflammatory drugs and anabolic hormones) and, in some instances, surgery to relieve the pressure on nervous tissues. Good nursing by the owner of the dog under veterinary advice is essential for the animal's recovery.

Skin problems

There are many kinds of skin disease that can affect dogs, and their diagnosis needs examination and often sample

---

COMMON SYMPTOMS
• **Thin or bald patches in the coat**
• **Scratching and licking**
• **Wet, dry or crusty sores.**

---

analysis by the vet. If you suspect skin problems, you must seek expert advice.

Healthy tips

The following useful tips will help to keep your dog's skin healthy and prevent any problems developing.
• Always feed your dog a balanced diet with sufficient fats

- Never apply any creams, powders or ointments without trimming back the dog's hair. Let oxygen get to the inflamed area
- Groom your dog regularly to keep his skin and coat healthy.

Mange

This can be caused by an invisible mite and can be seen as crusty, hairless sores. Fleas, lice and ticks also cause damage to a dog's coat (see page 104). If you see or suspect the presence of any of these skin parasites, you must obtain a specially formulated antiparasitic product from the pet shop, chemist or your vet and treat your dog immediately.

Treatment

Note that powders are of little use against mange, and drugs available in bath or aerosol form are much more appropriate. Tough, deep forms of mange, such as demodectic mange which is frequently complicated by the presence of secondary staphylococcal bacteria, may be treated by your veterinary surgeon using a combination of baths and drugs given by mouth. Jack Russell Terriers, particularly those types with smooth, short coats, are more prone than some other dog breeds to demodectic mange.

As there are several different types of mange, you should ask your veterinary surgeon to advise you on the best method of treating your particular case. With all anti-parasite treatment of skin diseases, it is extremely important that you follow the instructions on the label of the preparation being used.

Ringworm

This subtle ailment, to which Jack Russells seem predisposed, possibly because their immune system does not deal with the causal fungus efficiently and quickly, may require diagnosis by ultra-violet light examination or fungus culture from a hair specimen.

Special drugs, which are given by mouth or applied to the skin, are used for treating ringworm. However, great care must be taken to see that human contacts do not pick up the disease from the affected dog. Always wash your hands thoroughly after handling an affected animal.

Lumps and bumps

These may be abscesses, cysts or tumours and they may need surgical attention if they persist and grow larger. The earlier a growing lump is attended to, the simpler it is to eradicate, so you must always be sure to consult your vet by the time it reaches cherry size.

Hot spots

Sudden, sore, wet 'hot spots' that develop in the summer or autumn months may be caused by an allergy to pollen and other substances. Use some scissors to clip the hair over and round the affected area to a level with the skin, and then apply liquid paraffin. If your dog has hot spots, you should consult your veterinary surgeon as he may require anti-histamine or corticosteroid creams, injections or tablets. Although they tend to look dramatic, hot spots are quickly settled by treatment.

Nursing a sick dog

In all your dog's ailments, mild or serious, you will normally have to be prepared to do something to look after his welfare, usually acting in the capacity of nurse. This will involve learning some essential nursing techniques, such as how to take the animal's temperature and administer tablets and liquid medicines.

Be confident

When you are treating a sick dog always adopt a confident and positive approach. Be prepared and have everything ready in advance. Your dog will be reassured by your calmness.

Taking the temperature

You cannot rely on the state of a dog's nose as an effective indicator of his temperature, good health or sickness. As with children, being able to take your pet's temperature with a thermometer can help you to decide whether or not to call the vet and can also assist him in diagnosing and treating what is wrong.

You should use an ordinary glass thermometer, which you can purchase at most pharmacies. For preference, it should have a stubby rather than a slim bulb, or, better still, you can invest in an unbreakable thermometer, although these are more expensive. Lubricate the thermometer with a little olive oil or petroleum jelly and insert it about 2.5cm (1in) into the dog's rectum. Once it is in place, you can hold the thermometer with the bulb angled against the rectal wall for good contact. After half a minute, remove and read the thermometer.

A dog's normal temperature will be in the range of 38–38.6°C (101–101.6°F). Taking into account a slight rise for nervousness or excitement in some dogs, you can expect under such conditions to read up to 38.7°C (101.8°F) or even 38.8°C (102°F). Higher than that is abnormal. Shake down the mercury in the thermometer before use, and always be sure to clean and disinfect the instrument afterwards.

Administering medicine

Try to avoid putting medicines into your dog's food or drink, as this can be a very imprecise method. However, for dogs that are really averse to taking pills and capsules, you can conceal them in tasty titbits, but you must check that the dog has swallowed them.

Tablets, pills or capsules

These should always be dropped into the 'V'-shaped groove at the back of the dog's mouth while holding it open, with one thumb pressed firmly against the hard roof of the dog's mouth.

Liquids

These should always be given slowly, a little at a time, by the same method or direct into the dog's lip pouch with the mouth closed. They can be squirted through a syringe.

Handling your dog

It is very useful to know how to handle and restrain your dog effectively during visits to the vet, especially if he gets anxious about being examined or may even behave aggressively.

Making a makeshift muzzle

A muzzle is essential when a nervous, possessive, aggressive or sensitive dog is in pain and has to be handled or examined. To make one, you can use a length of bandage, string, nylon stocking or even a tie – it will prevent the owner and vet being bitten. By carefully positioning the muzzle not too far back, you can still administer liquid medicine by pouring it into the gap between the lips behind the encircling band.

1 Tie a knot in the bandage and wrap it around the dog's muzzle.
2 Cross the ends of the bandage at the bottom under the jaw.

3 Bring the ends round to the back of the dog's head and tie firmly.

At the vet's

It is important to know how to handle your dog when you visit the vet's surgery. Although some dogs trot in happily and do not mind being examined, others can be very nervous and may even panic. Very large dogs are usually looked at on the floor, but the vet will usually want to examine small to medium-sized dogs, such as Jack Russells, on the examination table and you will have to lift your dog up if so.

Lifting your dog

To avoid injury, not only to your dog but also to your back, always bend your knees when picking him up. Support his body properly with one hand on his chest between the front legs and the other below his rear or abdomen.

1 Get down and bend your knees and place one hand securely under your dog and the other one around his chest.

2 With your hand under the dog, taking most of his weight and holding him securely, rise up with your back straight.

3 Keep the dog in a secure position, holding him close to your body, as you bring him up to chest height.

First aid

First aid is the emergency care given to a dog suffering injury or illness of sudden onset. The aims of first aid are to keep the dog alive, to avoid any unnecessary suffering and prevent further injury.

Rules of first aid

- Always keep calm: if you panic, you will be unable to help the dog.
- Contact a vet as soon as possible: advice given over the phone may be life-saving
- Avoid any injury to yourself: a distressed or injured dog may bite, so use a muzzle if necessary
- Control any haemorrhage: excessive blood loss can lead to severe shock and even death
- Maintain an airway: failure to breathe or obtain adequate oxygen can lead to brain damage or loss of life.

Accidents and emergencies

In emergencies, your priorities are to keep your dog comfortable until he can be examined by a vet. However, in many cases, there is important action you can do immediately to help preserve your dog's health and life.

Burns

These can be caused by very hot liquids or by contact with an electrical current or various types of caustic, acid or irritant liquid. You must act quickly.

Electrical burns

Most electrical burns are the result of a dog chewing a live flex or cable, so wires should always be hidden, particularly from puppies, and electrical devices unplugged after use. Biting live wires can cause burns to the inside of the lips and the gums but may, in the worst cases, result in shock, collapse and death.

Recommended action First, switch off the electricity before you handle the patient. Examine the insides of the mouth and apply cold water to any burnt areas. If the gums are whiter than normal or blue-tinged, shock may be present. You must seek veterinary advice.

Chemical burns

Burns can also be caused by caustic chemicals, and you must seek veterinary attention if this happens.

Recommended action Wash the affected area with copious warm soapy water and then seek veterinary advice.

Scalding with a liquid

Hot water or oil spillage commonly occurs in the kitchen. Although the dog's coat affords him some insulating protection, the skin beneath may well be damaged with visible signs only emerging after several hours have passed in many cases.

Recommended action You must apply plenty of cold water immediately to the affected area and follow this by holding an ice pack on the burn – a bag of frozen peas is ideal. Then gently dry the burnt zone with mineral oil (liquid paraffin) and seek veterinary advice.

Poisoning

The house, the garden and the world outside contain a multitude of substances, both natural and artificial, that can poison a dog. If you suspect that your dog has been poisoned, you must contact your vet right away. Frequently some symptoms, such as vomiting, blood in the dog's stools or collapse, which owners may imagine to be the result of poisoning, are actually caused by other kinds of illness.

A dog may come into contact with poisonous chemicals through ingestion or by licking his coat when it is contaminated by a noxious substance. Canine inquisitiveness and the tendency to scavenge can lead dogs to eat or drink some strange materials. Sometimes owners will negligently give dangerous substances to their pets. Occasionally, poisonous gases or vapours are inhaled by animals. All our homes contain highly poisonous compounds. Poisoning can also be caused by certain plants, insect stings and the venom of snakes and toads.

Poisonous plants

Dangerous plants include the bulbs of many spring flowers, holly and mistletoe berries, the leaves and flowers of both rhododendrons and hydrangeas, leaves of yew, box and laurels, sweetpea, wisteria and bluebell seeds, and all parts of the columbine, hemlock, lily of the valley and ivy. Some fungi are as poisonous to

> **COMMON POISONS**
> - **Mouse and rat killer**
> - **Sleeping tablets**
> - **Carbon monoxide gas in faulty heaters and car exhausts**
> - **Weedkillers**
> - **Corrosive chemicals, such as acids, alkalis, bleach, carbolic acid, phenols, creosote and petroleum products**
> - **Antifreeze**
> - **Lead paint, solders, putty and fishing weights**
> - **Slug pellets**
> - **Insecticides**
> - **Rodenticides (warfarin)**
> - **Herbicides**
> - **Illegal bird baits**

dogs as they are to humans, as are the blue-green algae that sometimes bloom on garden ponds in hot weather. Keep your dog away from these plants.

> **COMMON SYMPTOMS**
> The symptoms of poisoning vary but they may be evident as:
> - **Digestive upsets, especially vomiting and diarrhoea**
> - **Difficulty in breathing**
> - **Convulsions**
> - **Uncoordinated movements or even coma.**
>
> Note: If any of these occur in your dog and you suspect poisoning, you must ring the vet immediately.

Recommended action Determining which poison is involved can be quite difficult if you don't know what the dog has come into contact with. Professional diagnostic methods at the earliest opportunity are vital.

1 Look for any evidence of burning or

blistering in the dog's mouth caused by corrosive poisons.
2 Flush out the mouth with warm water and let him drink water or milk.

Corrosive substances

1 Wipe clean the contaminated area with rags or paper tissues and cut off congealed masses of hair with scissors. Cooking oil or petroleum jelly will help soften paint and tar.
2 Wash thoroughly with dog or baby shampoo and rinse well. Don't use paint thinners, concentrated washing detergents, solvents or turpentine.
Note: If the poison has been swallowed recently (within one hour), try to make the dog vomit by giving him either a chunk of washing soda (sodium carbonate) the size of a large pea or some English mustard powder (half a teaspoon in a quarter cup of water).

Bee and wasp stings

Painful, but usually single and with no serious general effects, insect stings require little more than removal of the sting itself in the case of bee stings (wasps and hornets do not leave their stings behind) by means of tweezers and the application of antihistamine cream. Rarely, death can ensue if a dog is subject to a large number, perhaps hundreds, of stings. Stings can also be serious if the tongue or mouth are involved.

> **COMMON SYMPTOMS**
> • The dog's throat will swell
> • If he is allergic to the insect venom, he will go into severe shock.

Recommended action If your dog goes into shock, he will need anti-shock therapy, such as intravenous fluids, adrenalin and antihistamine injections. Keep him warm and make sure that his breathing is unimpeded while you obtain veterinary attention.

Snake bites

Britain's only venomous snake, the common adder, may sometimes bite a dog who disturbs it.

> **COMMON SYMPTOMS**
> • Two tiny slit-like punctures in the skin, which rapidly become surrounded by a zone of swollen reaction
> • Tremble, salivating, vomiting and staggering
> • The dog may then go into shock and collapse or even die.

Recommended action You must take the dog straight to the vet for treatment with adder anti-venom – do not delay.

Bleeding

The appearance of blood anywhere on a dog's body necessitates immediate close inspection. A variety of accidents and some diseases may produce blood from the nostrils, eyes or ears or in the droppings or in vomited material. None of the above types of haemorrhage are usually suitable for first aid by the owner. All need veterinary attention, however, though the causes may often be trivial and ephemeral.

Bleeding from the body surface through wounds inflicted during fights, traffic accidents or other traumatic incidents can be copious, and this does require prompt first aid.

Recommended action The most important thing you can do is to apply pressure to the wound. Hand or finger pressure is always invaluable until a pad of gauze or cotton wool can be found. This should be soaked in cold water, placed on the wound and kept in place by constant firm pressure or, better still, a bandage. Take the dog to a veterinary surgery as quickly as possible. Do not waste any time applying antiseptic ointments or powders to a significantly bleeding wound.

Heat stroke

Every summer we read in the newspapers of cases of dogs dying from heat stroke as a result of the gross thoughtlessness and negligence of their owners. Just like babies and young children, dogs who are left in hot, poorly ventilated spaces, particularly cars, and sometimes without water, will overheat.

COMMON SYMPTOMS
- **Inability to control internal body temperature**
- **As the latter rises, the dog will become distressed, pant rapidly and will quickly weaken**
- **The dog's mouth will appear much redder than normal**
- **Collapse, coma and even death can follow in a reasonably short space of time, so you must act quickly.**

Recommended action Cooling the affected dog's body, particularly his head, by means of cold water baths, hosing and ice packs is essential.

If the temperature-regulating mechanism in the brain has already been seriously damaged a fatal outcome may still ensue. Veterinary attention must be obtained immediately. Of course, by being a responsible and thoughtful owner, you can prevent such emergencies occurring.

Foreign bodies

These can occur in various parts of a dog's anatomy and the treatment will vary according to the location.

In the eye

Foreign bodies in the eye will cause the dog to rub his head on the ground and paw at his eye.

Recommended action Flood the affected eye with human-type eye drops or olive oil to float out the foreign body. Do not use tweezers close to the eyeball.

In the ear

Plant seeds and grass awns are particularly likely to get into a dog's ears during summer walks. Their presence causes itching and irritation. The dog will shake his head and scratch and paw at his ears.

Recommended action Pour some warm olive oil or other vegetable oil into the ear, filling it. The object may float to the surface and can then be picked up by fine tweezers. Deeper, embedded foreign bodies will always require veterinary attention.

In the mouth

Pieces of bone or splinters of wood can become lodged in a dog's mouth. The offending object may be jammed between the left and right upper molars at the back of the mouth or between two adjacent teeth. Less commonly, an object, such as a small ball, can get stuck in a dog's throat. In all cases, he will show symptoms of distress, including pawing at the mouth, gagging, trying to retch or shaking his head.

Recommended action While someone holds the dog firmly, you should open his mouth and try to dislodge the foreign body with a spoon or kitchen tongs. Where the dog is having difficulty breathing and literally choking, try holding him upside down, massaging the throat and slapping his back. If you cannot remove the object, you must seek veterinary help at once.

In the paws
Splinters of glass, thorns, particles of metal and even fragments of stone can penetrate the pads on a dog's paws or lodge in the skin between the toes. As a result, the dog limps and usually licks the affected paw.

Recommended action If the object is visible, you can remove it with tweezers. If not, because of being embedded, then bathe the foot two to three times daily in warm water and salt (a teaspoon of salt to a cupful of water) until the foreign body emerges from the softened skin. If lameness persists for more than a day or two, seek veterinary attention as infection may set in.

Fish hooks
You must never attempt to pull out a fish hook, wherever it is. Instead, use a pair of pliers to cut the end of the fish hook and then carefully push the barbed end out through the skin. If it looks sore, rub in antiseptic cream.

Useful information

Organizations

Association of Pet Behaviour Counsellors
PO Box 46
Worcester WR8 9YS
tel: 01386 751151
www.apbc.org.uk

British Veterinary Association
7 Mansfield Street
London W1M 0AT
tel: 020 7636 6541
www.bva.co.uk

DEFRA
Ergon House, c/o Nobel House
17 Smith Square
London SW1P 3JR
tel: 020 7238 6951
www.defra.gov.uk

The Kennel Club
1–5 Clarges Street
Piccadilly
London W1Y 8AB
tel: 0870 606 6750
www.thekennelclub.org.uk

Magazines

Dog World
www.dogworld.co.uk

Dogs Monthly
www.dogsmonthly.co.uk

Dogs Today
www.dogstodaymagazine.co.uk

Our Dogs
www.ourdogs.co.uk

Your Dog
www.yourdog.co.uk

Websites

Animal Health Trust
www.aht.org.uk

Association of Pet Dog Trainers
www.apdt.co.uk

Company of Animals Clicker Training
www.companyofanimals.co.uk

Jack Russell Terrier Club of Great Britain
www.jackrussellgb.co.uk

Jack Russells Online
www.jackrussells.com

National Dog Tattoo Register
www.dog-register.co.uk

Parson Russell Terrier Club
www.parsonrussellterrierclub.co.uk

Pet Care Trust
www.petcare.org.uk

Pet Health Care
www.PEThealthcare.co.uk

Petlog
www.thekennelclub.org.uk/meet/petlog.html

Royal College of Veterinary Surgeons
www.rcvs.org.uk

Index

Index